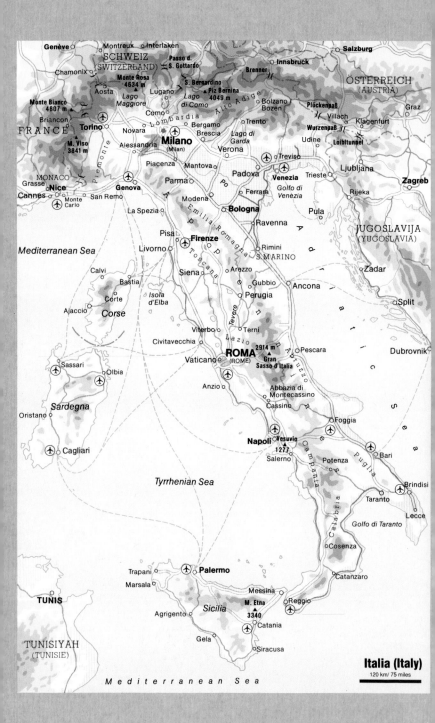

Italia (Italy)
120 km/ 75 miles

INSIGHT *Pocket* GUIDES

MILAN

Written and Presented by **Umberto Troni**

INSIGHT
Pocket
GUIDES

Insight Pocket Guide:

MILAN

Directed by
Hans Höfer

Editorial Director
Andrew Eames

Editor
Joachim Beust

Photography by
Sergio Piumatti

Design Concept by
V. Barl

Design by
Gaia Text

© **1993 APA Publications (HK) Ltd**

All Rights Reserved

Printed in Singapore by
Höfer Press (Pte) Ltd
Fax: 65-8616438

Distributed in the United States by
Houghton Mifflin Company
2 Park Street
Boston, Massachusetts 02108
ISBN: 0-395-65766-0

Distributed in Canada by
Thomas Allen & Son
390 Steelcase Road East
Markham, Ontario L3R 1G2
ISBN: 0-395-65766-0

Distributed in the UK & Ireland by
GeoCenter International UK Ltd
The Viables Center, Harrow Way
Basingstoke, Hampshire RG22 4BJ
ISBN: 9-62421-553-7

Worldwide distribution enquiries:
Höfer Communications Pte Ltd
38 Joo Koon Road
Singapore 2262
ISBN: 9-62421-553-7

Benvenuti !

Welcome! When Giorgio Strehler, the famous theatre director, invited me to Milan to work with him as director in his Piccolo Teatro, I couldn't believe my luck. I, a Venetian, had long been an admirer of Milan. When I got out of the train I was overwhelmed straight away by the sight of the huge Stazione Centrale, which wouldn't look out of place as scenery for Verdi's *Aida* – which after all had its birth in this city. Even today, Milan still makes my pulse race.

After Venice, it wasn't easy adapting to the feverish, relentless work ethic: Milan is one enormous factory in which human energy gets released from dawn until dusk. I wanted to get to know this city intimately, and I did it the way I know best – by bicycle. I've pedalled everywhere and discovered hundreds of little 'villages', parts of the city where people of widely differing backgrounds come together.

Milan isn't just a city of work, it also contains magnificent works of art – though it doesn't show off about them, as Rome and Florence do. On my itineraries you'll get to know the magnificent Duomo, La Scala, basilicas, *palazzi*, medieval squares and streets, Roman ruins, secret corners and above all the people of Milan themselves. I have also devised excursions that will take you out of town, to the stately medieval towns of Bergamo and Pavia, amongst others. In addition, I have provided you with my own selection of restaurants and shops – tried and tested, I assure you! At the back of the book is all the practical information you could possibly need.

At this juncture I would like to thank my Milanese friends who have been so selfless in their help. This book is dedicated to them: Eugenia and Glauco Carmagnani, Giacomo and Rosanna Pellegrini, Marinella and Elia Mangoni – and of course my wife Ima Agustoni, a television actress well known to the Italian public. It was she who taught me that famous Milanese dialect song, *Oh mia bèla Madunina,* which celebrates the beauty of the city and its people. — Umberto Troni.

Contents

Practical Information

HISTORY

The City in the Middle

Milan, or Milano, derives its name from the Celtic 'mid land', and the city's origins stretch back to the 4th century BC when the Celtic tribe of the Insubres conquered northern Italy.

The Romans, who conquered Milan under Consul Marcus Claudius Marcellus in 222BC, named the place 'Mediolanum', because Milan, strategically situated as it is in the Padana Plain, links the Italian peninsula and continental Europe. Milan thus became an important military base on the north-western border of the Roman province

Leonardo da Vinci, 'Musico'

of Cisalpine Gaul, which soon expanded to include the whole of Upper Italy.

The collapse of the Roman Empire into its two halves meant that Milan acquired the status of capital of the Western Roman Empire between AD286 and 402. It was the second largest city in Italy after Rome itself. Moreover, the Emperor Constantine's Edict of Milan, issued in 313, made the city the capital of Western Christendom; and after the arrival of St Ambrose from Trier, Milan played a decisive role in the Catholic Church's dispute with the Arians.

Archaeological finds at S Sepolcro

Culture

and in the Via Nerino, as well as at the Porta Romana and the Porta Ticinese, reveal that the Roman city was originally laid out in the form of a square.

After the fall of Rome, in the 6th century, the epoch of the Lombards began; however, their kings chose Pavia as their capital, and Monza as their summer residence. And Milan? Three centuries later, in 1176, it was once again very prominent and in a position to inflict defeat on the emperor Barbarossa. During this period the Basilica of S Ambrogio was rebuilt and served as a model for every other Romanesque structure in Italy – the Basilica of S Eustorgio and the Abbazia di Chiaravalle being just two examples.

Antonio Pollaiolo, 'giovane donna'

At the end of the 13th century, the Visconti family and its heirs became the supreme lords of Milan. The city grew rich and the Gothic architecture of the *Duomo*, the cathedral, became a symbol of Milan's revival. The city's trading connections extended across Europe to London – Lombard Street dates from that time.

In the mid-15th century the Sforza family took over from the Viscontis and began constructing the Castello Sforzesco. Milan reached the high point of its prosperity during this period, and attracted famous artists such as Leonardo da Vinci and Bramante.

At the end of the 15th century Milan fell to the French, and in 1525 to the Spanish-Austrian Habsburg empire of Charles V, whose financier, Tommaso Marino, began the palace in the Piazza della Scala (today it is the seat of the municipal authorities) in 1539.

In 1565 the Milanese archbishop S Carlo Borromeo created the

11

The Piazza della Scala around 1880

very first social institution for the poor of the city, while Federico Borromeo laid the foundations of the famous Pinacoteca Ambrosiana. In 1630 the city suffered an outbreak of the plague.

In 1714, after the Peace of Rastatt, which brought the War of the Spanish Succession to an end, Milan became part of Austria. The Milanese bourgeoisie developed, craft and manufacturing flourished and the city was once again visited by great artists: Tiepolo, for example, who did the frescoes for the Palazzo Clerici. Austrian empress Maria Theresa promoted the arts and created an efficient administration. The Accademia di Brera, the Orto Botanico and the Osservatorio Astronomico were all established. The Teatro alla Scala was the masterpiece of Neoclassical architect Piermarini; Maggiolini started the Milanese tradition of furniture design, and dell'Appiani created frescoes to adorn the houses of the wealthy.

In 1796 Napoleon occupied Milan and built the Foro Buonaparte and the Arco della Pace. In 1815, after the Congress of Vienna, the Austrians returned again and stayed until 1859. During these years the Italian liberation movement known as the *Risorgimento* found its fullest expression in the operas of Giuseppe Verdi, which were a huge success at La Scala.

After the unification of Italy, Milan became the industrial, financial and pragmatic capital of Italy. It began to outgrow its 17th-century Spanish walls. The first workers' tenements sprang up to the north, around the factories of Falk, Breda and Pirelli, and work began on such monumental public buildings as the central station and the city cemetery. The old canals, the *navigli*, were filled in, and the first ring-roads were built above them.

After World War I the focus of industrial development shifted away from metalworking and rubber to the automobile industry, Alfa Romeo, Isotta Fraschini, Bianchi, and Magneti Marelli being just some of the sonorous names. In a climate marked by strikes and lockouts, and by clashes between workers and employers, the Partito Nazionale Fascista, founded by Benito Mussolini in 1919 and financed by industry, gained ground steadily and eventually came to power in 1924. During the Fascist period the city expanded rapidly, and in 1943 it numbered one million inhabitants.

At the end of World War II, Milan very soon reassumed its leading economic role. New housing estates and office blocks – the Stazione Garibaldi is a typical example – were built in the areas of the city that had been destroyed. The Pirelli building, erected in 1955, is the symbol of this rebirth.

In the wake of this economic development, Milan became a popular destination for immigrants from Southern Italy. Luchino Visconti's film *Rocco and his Brothers* portrays the difficulties encountered by a rural family attempting to adapt to the alien world of the big city. This influx of new social groups contributed greatly to the 'Italian economic miracle' of the 1960s. It was also during these years that the Piccolo Teatro of Giorgio Strehler and Paolo Grassi first began to make a name for itself.

By the end of the 1960s, Milan's destiny was being shaped by political struggles. The so-called 'hot autumn' of the trade unions in 1968 was followed by the *anni di piombo*, or 'leaden years', during which the struggle of the *Brigate Rosse* (Red Brigade) against the 'system' reached its climax with the death of the publisher Feltrinelli. Himself a supporter of the terrorist left, Feltrinelli died while attempting to blow up a high-voltage transmission tower.

After this, municipal policy was determined by various coalitions under the leadership of mostly socialist mayors. In the 1980s Milan's economic development gained speed once more, and the city assumed a leading role as the nation's economy shifted towards an emphasis on service structures (trade, finance, information, fashion, design, advertising, publishing and the mass media). The city's historic centre, once bounded by the *navigli*, lost 300,000 inhabitants between 1974 and 1990. Today only 1.4 million Milanese live here, though if one includes the surrounding areas the population of Milan numbers more than 4 million.

Centro Direzionale

Milan's task for the 1990s is to reconcile powerful and conflicting financial and speculative interests, above all with regard to deciding on new locations for headquarters of firms in the services sector. Civic policy is largely determined by lobbyists from the political parties, large financial holdings and state firms. Hopefully the practical and constructive mind of the Milanese will retain the upper hand even in this delicate situation, and succeed in preserving the city's humanity.

The Future of Milan

Although the population of the urban heart of Milan has been decreasing since the mid-1970s, Greater Milan, *la grande Milano*, is clearly becoming more congested. Thirty years ago this conurbation was still a flourishing agricultural area, but today the 200 municipalities that make up the *Provincia di Milan*, and which have since been absorbed by the big city, are suffering from the resulting infrastructural problems. Because of their administrative fragmentation and political structure, none of them is in a position to organise an efficient public services system. The Milan Metro, with barely 50km (30 miles) of rail, is totally unable to cater for any meaningful portion of the city's 500,000 or so daily commuters. Nor are there enough bus and taxi lanes. The result: streets jammed with private cars, queues everywhere, stress and smog. Since the 1970s, Milan's city council has repeatedly failed to get its development plans – which rarely leave the drawing board anyway – approved by the surrounding municipalities. Indeed, Milan's satellite towns, which have sprung up to the south of the city as if by magic during the last 20 years, are less the result of planning initiative than of real estate speculation. Predictably, none of these new towns is connected to the city's public transport network: expressways lead directly into the city centre instead.

The busy Corso Buenos Aires

Meanwhile, the population in the city's historic centre has increasingly had to make way for new offices and apartment blocks. Milan's famous and traditional hotels are being transformed into luxury residences housing the top managers of the city's big firms, who pay astronomical rents to stay there, while their families enjoy fresh air and tranquillity out in their villas on Lake Como – all of them luxury commuters who drive out of the city at weekends, when others are not driving in. This phenomenon of 'the exodus of the rich' – actually quite a recent development – has meant that Milan has lost a lot of taxation revenue, since people here are taxed according to where they live. Even major firms such as Pirelli, Alfa Romeo and Magneti Marelli – Milan's pride and joy as well as the city's main sources of revenue – are relocating outside the city, where they can create their own efficient infrastructures themselves: IBM alone has provided 2,200 jobs in Segrate, to the northwest of the city.

In the not-so-distant future it is possible that Milan, beset by explosive immigration problems, will not have enough means at its disposal to stem the tide of inner-city misery that is such a feature of so many other large cities the world over.

Historical Highlights

6 BC Milan founded by the Etruscans.

396 BC Celtic tribe of the Insubres overruns the original Etruscan settlement.

222 BC Milan taken by Rome.

AD 286–402 Milan becomes capital of the Western Roman Empire.

313 Constantine the Great issues the Edict of Milan, granting tolerance of the Christian faith.

374 St Ambrose elected bishop of Milan.

1097 Birth of the *Comune di Milano*, Free City of Milan with its own independent charter.

1162 Milan captured by Barbarossa.

1176 The Lombard League, founded in 1167, composed of the cities of Upper Italy and led by Milan, defeats Barbarossa near Legnano.

1277 The Viscontis become the lords of Milan. Their coat-of-arms portrays a serpent with a Saracen in its mouth.

1450 Francesco Sforza, son-in-law of the last of the Viscontis, is made Duke of Milan. The city then flourishes under Ludovico Sforza, 'Il Moro' (1479–99).

1499 Milan occupied by the French under Louis XII.

1525 After the victory of Charles V over the French near Pavia, Milan becomes part of the Habsburg empire.

1556 Partition of the Habsburg empire: the Duchy of Milan becomes the property of Philip II of Spain.

1630 Outbreak of the plague in the city, vividly described by 19th-century writer Alessandro Manzoni.

1714 War of the Spanish Succession ends. Milan becomes part of Austria, and flourishes under Empress Maria Theresa.

1796 Milan occupied by Napoleon.

1815 Milan becomes Austrian again after the Congress of Vienna. The *Risorgimento*, and the flowering of Milanese opera and theatre, gathers pace.

1859 Milan becomes Italian. The city becomes the nation's industrial and financial capital.

1918 By the end of World War I, the city has 700,000 inhabitants. First labour disputes take place, led by *Partito Socialista* of Turati and Anna Kulischoff.

1919 In the Piazza San Sepolcro, Mussolini announces the foundation of the Fascist Party. Marinetti's Futurism triumphs in the artistic salons. One of the most famous painters in this movement, Tullio Crali, is still alive today.

1924–40 The city's population rises to one million during the years of Fascism.

1943 Milan suffers serious damage during Allied bombing raids. First *piani regolatori*, development plans, are drawn up for the city.

1946 Milan once again becomes the capital of Italian industry.

1955 The Pirelli building, symbol of the city's reconstruction, is erected.

1957 Construction work begins on the Milan Metro. Lack of town planning leads to the destruction of old parts of the city. Dormitory suburbs spring up, unfortunately not connected to the Metro.

1968 Student unrest, and the 'hot autumn' of the trade unions.

1970s Red Brigade terrorism.

1982 Economic revival. The age of information dawns.

1990 Political-administrative crisis in the Milan city council. The issue of restructuring the city – choosing where to relocate the centres of the new economic development – leads to fierce conflicts between private and public interests. 1.4 million Milanese live in the municipal area; a total of 4 million live in greater Milan.

Understanding Milan

Anyone who understands Milan understands Italy. Far more than Rome, Florence, Venice or Naples, Milan is a true cross-section of all things Italian, with its magnificent historical and cultural heritage, its cultural and human interest, its urbanity and its architecture. Milan may be defined as the 'pragmatic' capital of Italy; and it is also the most European of all Italy's cities. A permanent rival to Rome, the political capital, Milan remains the reference point for Italy. While Rome discusses, Milan acts. But Rome does create the economic framework within which Milan has to act, much to the grief of many Milanese managers forced to commute to Rome and haunt its antechambers in order to obtain permits and licences.

View from the Duomo

Milan is the centre of high finance and of economic and industrial power. It is also the headquarters of the country's private television stations, its press and advertising agencies and its fashion designers. On top of that, the city also possesses the best higher education establishments and the best university structures in Italy.

Milan is laid out in the shape of a star around the Duomo, and its industrial and suburban sprawl extends out towards Como, Varese and Monza in the northwest and towards Bergamo in the northeast. The city has also spread southwards over the past few years, evidenced by the weird-looking skyscraper estates at Gratosoglio or the small garden cities of Milano Fiori or San Siro.

Even though the construction work in the city is often bad – a result of the administration's frequent failure to punish contraventions of land utilization or building plans – its historical quarters still retain their character.

The visitor will be amazed by the sheer tempo of everyday business life here, and by the inimitable ease with which festivals are celebrated. Evenings tend to be spent in the city's 50 cinemas, in its 45 theatres where plays, music and cabaret can be enjoyed, or in its literary cafés, its typical *osterie* (bars) and its discothèques. Particularly good places to go are the Piazza del Duomo, Corso Vittorio Emanuele, Via Torino, the Brera, and the area around the Porta Ticinese.

Immigrants add to the cosmopolitan feel of Milan: Black Africans, North Africans, Philippinos and Chinese work as domestic staff, sell smuggled cigarettes on street-cor-

Rooftops in the Navigli area

ners and also run small shops selling exotic goods. Out in the suburbs clashes between locals and – often illegal – immigrants are on the increase. But sooner or later this new workforce will be integrated too; Milan has always understood how to learn from its immigrants, how to live from the ideas and the energy of those eager to work.

Milan never stands still, it keeps on changing and renewing itself, and that applies not only to urban development here but also to the lifestyle of its inhabitants. Look the Milan of today in the face and you'll sense the eagerness with which it faces tomorrow.

Understanding the Milanese

A lot of cities welcome strangers with open arms; more prejudiced ones reject them. Milan rather tends to put its freshly-arrived visitor to the test and, if he passes, accepts him. Should he fail, however, he gets rejected.

The Milanese are open-hearted, cheerful, outspoken and very helpful. This is why we recommend the visitor to be both kind and inquisitive. The search for knowledge is the fount of creativity, and it's almost sacred as far as the Milanese are concerned. Adapt yourself to the Milanese and you're sure to be readily accepted.

The Milanese are intuitive and generous. The expression *El milanès el ga el cör in man* (rough translation: 'the Milanese wears his heart on his sleeve') didn't originate by accident. The people are also thoroughly reliable, both at work and in private. A visitor who is open and has nothing to hide will discover an equally open and many-sided Milan. For this reason Milan can be regarded as the only really cosmopolitan city in all Italy – a genuine melting-pot.

A genuine Milanese

The city has changed enormously over the past 20 years. The industrial era is long gone, and with its service-based so-

True service

ciety Milan is now at the cutting edge of European progress.

The average Milanese gets out of bed at 6.30am, drinks a *caffé espresso* (very few Italians have a proper breakfast), and then listens to the news in the bathroom, paying special attention to the Tokyo stock market report (the Milanese adore stocks and shares). Then it's off to work, bumper to bumper, into the smog and stress (every morning 300,000 drive in, 90,000 drive out); the Metro only slightly alleviates the situation, and the buses get stuck in the traffic jams too.

And every morning there's the *vigile del traffico, 'Il Ghisa'*, the traffic policeman, with his elegant uniform and elegant gestures, setting things right with shrill blows on his whistle. *Ghisa* is a nickname, so do avoid saying *scusi, signor Ghisa* to him; the correct version is *scusi signor vigile*.

The *Ghisa* is both loved and feared, and this becomes most evident during *Epifania* (Epiphany) when the Milanese, who have received mountains of traffic tickets throughout the year, heap up great piles of *panettoni* (Milanese cake with lemon rind and sultanas added) at the feet of the aforesaid guardian of the law as he stands at his road junction, to thank him for the difficult and wearing task he is forced to perform. That's typical of the Milanese: they're generous and *simpatico*.

Daily at midday, the hectic rush spreads to the bars: people eat standing up in a *tavola calda*, though not without having had a swift *aperitivo* beforehand. The bars in Milan provide all kinds of different snacks – olives, *crostini al salmone, crostini alle verdure, patatine* – all of which can be accompanied by a Campari, a Zucca, a Martini or a Prosecco. Conversation revolves inescapably around the *Weekend*: the seaside, the mountains, the holiday home, skiing, sailing, Paris, or the latest exhibition in Venice or Florence. The Milanese are always on the move, and eager to

Time for a Campari

see things, experience things – the very act of travelling is relaxation for them!

Then in the evening there's *cena alla casa* (supper at home), or in a restaurant with friends. Parents stay at home in front of the television, the young are drawn out to the *caffé* and the *discoteche*. Some people visit *La Scala*, the world famous Milan opera, or the *Piccolo*, the 'Little Theatre', still the number one theatrical venue in Milan thanks to Giorgio Strehler.

The social structure of the city is, however, not as homogeneous as it once was. These days the Milanese are protesting, not against the *immigranti* who provide their own problems, but against the municipal administration which is treating the phenomenon of immigration with apparent indifference, and seems to have no plan for coping with the need to find jobs and accommodation for the newcomers.

Getting your Bearings

Milan is laid out in the shape of a star, with the Piazza del Duomo at its centre. The old ring of the *navigli* – ancient canals which were once navigable, but are now filled in – once used to surround the medieval city.

A second ring, laid out when the walls dating from the Spanish period were torn down, reveals the extent of urban expansion in the 16th century, though it also encompasses the green open spaces of the Parco Sempione and the Giardini Pubblici.

Most of what happens in Milan takes place within these two rings. Taking centre stage are the Piazza del Duomo, the Galleria Vittorio Emanuele and the area between Via Dante, Via Manzoni and Corso Vittorio Emanuele. But the extension of the latter, the Corso Venezia, which continues on beyond the Porta Venezia to become the amazingly straight Corso Buenos Aires (and later, at the Piazzale Loreto, leads on to the motorways heading north), also plays a leading role in the world of elegance, fashion, industry and high finance which together go to make up the fabric of Italy's second city.

The northern part of the city is its industrial heart, while the south is predominantly residential, with such satellite towns as Milano Fiori and Milano 3 in Basiglio.

Day itineraries

DAY 1

The Old City

From the Gothic pinnacles of Milan's Duomo to the music of Verdi in La Scala. This is a day's itinerary on foot, beginning at the Piazza del Duomo, and continuing via the Palazzo Reale, the Museo del Duomo, the Galleria Vittorio Emanuele, the Teatro della Scala and the Museo Poldi-Pozzoli, to the Palazzo Clerici.

– Tram 1, 4, 8, 15, 19, 24, bus 65, Metro M2/3 –

For all of us here in Milan the **Duomo** is far more than just a church: it is a symbol of the city, and the Madonnina on top of its highest pinnacle, shining golden against the sky, accompanies every

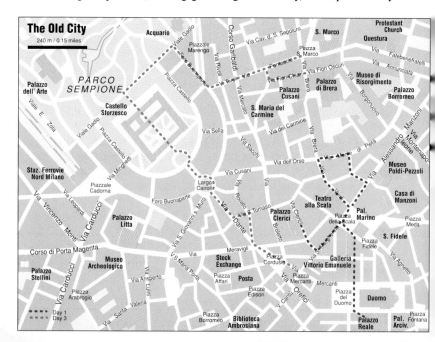

The Old City

240 m / 0.15 miles

- - - Day 1
- - - Day 3

Milanese on his travels – *O mia bella Madunina*. The massive cathedral nevertheless conveys a strong sense of lightness, especially because of those pinnacles decorating its facade. Work on the Duomo began in 1386 and has never really stopped since: the Milanese refer to their cathedral very aptly as the 'factory', because the last of its five gigantic bronze doors, the work of sculptor Minguzzi, was only finally completed in 1965. If you include the highest pinnacle it is 109m (350ft) high, 157m (500ft) long and 92m (300ft) wide. Built of pink-tinged Italian marble (which has only recently been liberated from its grey coating of exhaust fumes), the Duomo is the third largest church in Christendom after St Peter's in Rome and Seville cathedral. It can house more than 25,000 people. There are over 3,000 statues clustered together on the facade and on the roof, and you need to go up 500 steps in order to reach the terrace – don't worry though: lifts are also available (look for the sign saying *ascensori* at the left-hand entrance).

Milan's Duomo and the Madonnina

Structural alterations, above all during the 15th century at the hands of S Carlo Borromeo, have not detracted from the sheer splendour of its Gothic architecture. You will be overawed by the majesty interior of the Duomo, and if you sit alone in the half-darkness of one of the five naves and let your gaze wander across the milky light penetrating the magnificent windows, and along the mighty columns all the way up to the ceiling – if possible during a celebration of early morning mass – you will understand something of the overpowering mystery of the place.

The **Treasury** (*Tesuro del Duomo,* admission 1000 lire) is situated on the right-hand side of the rear choir. Archbishop Ariberto's Evangeliary can be admired here. The chapel of S Carlo Borromeo is also worth a visit – the gold mask on the sarcophagus is particularly impressive.

Keep an eye out for an astronomical curiosity: from the left nave, where a sundial with a Capricorn symbol can be seen, a narrow brass strip runs across the floor, crossing the entire cathedral and ending on the right side. Light falls directly on this strip through a hole in the roof twice annually, on 21 June and 21 December, and the system was once used to keep time.

To reach the roof, first take the lift and then continue upwards on foot until you finally reach the feet of the Madonnina. Here it's easy to get lost among the 700-year-old pinnacles, and there's a fantastic view of the city and the nearby Alps to be had – only on certain days, however, when the wind is in the right direction, otherwise the Milanese panorama tends, unfortunately, to be cloaked in a comparatively thick layer of smog.

Back down at the bottom, you can begin your walk through central Milan. To be perfectly honest, the **Piazza del Duomo** really is rather ugly: the 1943 bombardment destroyed nearly all of the old buildings around the cathedral square. Today's building facades are, moreover, 'adorned' by even more unpleasant-looking neon signs. And Mussolini's ugly Palazzo dell'Arengario, situated right next to the majestic Duomo, clashes dreadfully with it. However, the Palazzo dell'Arengario does contain the **Tourist Information Office**, *Azienda Promozione Turismo APT* (open 9am–6pm), where you can find brochures and information.

Behind the Arengario is the **Palazzo Reale**, built by Piermarini, the architect of La Scala. This building, commissioned in 1770 by the Austrian empress Maria Theresa, today houses magnificent exhibitions, and also contains the **Museo Civico d'Arte Contemporanea** (open daily except Monday 9.30am–12.30pm and 2.30–5.20pm). Having taken a look at the extensive collection of contemporary

Galleria Vittorio Emanuele

Italian art and sculpture here it's worth going back to the cathedral once more to visit the **Museo del Duomo** (daily 9.30am–12.30pm and 3.30–6pm, admission 3,000 lire). Here, an informative and extensive collection, covering 20 exhibition rooms, documents the history of the building.

Afterwards you must bid farewell to the pigeons and the Japanese tourists, as well as to Vittorio Emanuele II on his horse in the middle of the square, and plunge into the world of the **Galleria Vittorio Emanuele**, the finest and most exclusive shopping arcade in all of Italy. The southernmost of the Galleria's four 'arms' connects the Duomo with La Scala. Here you'll find numbers of super-chic shops and 'in' restaurants along a distance of 200m (650ft). And it's in the Galleria that you can have your first *aperitivo* of the day – a sacred ritual, performed once before lunch and once before going home in the evening. On the corner, on the left of the entrance to the Duomo, is the famous **Camparino**; it is named after the Campari family, inventors of the aperitif. So, how would you like your Campari: straight *(liscio)*, or with soda *(al Selz)*? No question about it: Campari definitely needs to be drunk with soda, but first the glass gets 'dunked' in finely-chopped ice. Preparing a Campari in this way is a real art: watch carefully how the barman does it so that you can practise at home later on!

The Duomo, Campari, Alfa Romeo and Pirelli are famed throughout the world. But what about La Scala, the world's most famous opera house? It, surely, is the true symbol of Milan. Approach it via the northern exit of the Galleria. On the way there, in the centre of the Galleria, you will pass the most famous restaurant in Milan, **Il Savini**. The cuisine in this highly traditional restaurant is superb, and the service excellent. Daytime customers should wear jackets and ties, and in the evening, dark suits.

La Scala programme

Opposite is a culinary trauma: the former traditional restaurant of **Il Biffi** now houses a fast-food outlet. It really is a travesty that the city gave this place a licence – especially considering the fact that the Town Hall is only a few steps away, and that the Mayor himself is forced to witness this eyesore daily!

La Scala! And the magic of music, whether Verdi, Rossini, Puccini, Wagner, Toscanini or Karajan, Callas or Pavarotti. On your first visit it's best to get tickets for the cheap seats high up in the gallery *(loggione)*. It's here that you see the real music-lovers, the ones who arrive with scores tucked under their arms and know every note and every breath of the primadonna by heart. It's these people who really give life to La Scala. Every year on 7 December rich financiers' wives wear unbelievable dresses for the season's opening.

Take up your position at the foot of the statue of Leonardo da Vinci on the Piazza della Scala and admire the world's first ever opera house, built on the site of the former church of S Maria della Scala by Piermarini in 1777–78. Were it not for its contents the simple-looking facade would be easy to pass by. During a winter's day, I suggest you take a seat in the **Caffé del Biffi Scala** and watch all the ballerinas and singers running by, wrapped up snugly in warm cashmere scarves for fear of catching cold. And in the evenings there is the elegant, yet all too human crush at the entrances to the building. Black marketeers thrive here. A piece of advice: give your hotel doorman a good tip and he should be able to get hold of a ticket for you.

The **Museo della Scala** (open 10am–12 noon and 3–5pm, closed Monday) offers a rewarding look behind the scenes of this venerable institution.

To the right of La Scala is the elegant **Via Manzoni**, with its array of the most exclusive shops in Milan. But first there is just one more museum you should visit, the **Museo Poldi Pezzoli** (open daily 9.30am–12.30pm and 2.30–6pm), a treasure-trove of Milanese culture full of valuable paintings, porcelain and carpets.

Your route continues along the Via Manzoni before turning left into the Via Romagnosi, a pretty little street with its sturdy and severely elegant *palazzi*. Now you are in the Via Monte di Pietà, which contains the Monte dei Pegni, a famous pawnbroker's shop visited by every social class, including society women. They transfer their fur coats here every summer, and the coats are carefully looked after in a refrigerator until the winter. This is useful because it keeps them out of the way, the pawn money comes in very handy, and after all, their husbands are sure to redeem the furs once the season begins again.

Now continue to the junction of the Via Verdi which will take you back to the Piazza della Scala, and from there follow the Via S Margherita, turning right into the Via Clerici to reach the **Palazzo Clerici**. This magnificent 18th-century Milanese patrician's house contains a real treasure: the banqueting hall known as the **Galleria degli Arezzi** with its fantastic barrel vault and its 119 sq. metres (1,280 sq. ft) of fresco by Tiepolo – the Venetian painter's greatest work. The Palazzo today houses a study centre for international politics. Ask politely at the porter's lodge to be let in.

Milanese like to talk

You've reached the end of your stroll for today. From the Via Clerici it's just a stone's throw to the Galleria again. How about a visit to Savini restaurant? You're not wearing a jacket and tie? Then cross the Piazza del Duomo and have a swift bite to eat in the **Duomo Center**. Service or self-service: the choice is yours.

In the evening you can visit **La Scala** with the ticket you bought during the day, or go to a concert at the **Conservatorio** (Via Conservatorio 12, Tel: 760 017 55). Or try a play at the **Teatro dell'Elfo** (Via Menotti 11, Tel: 71 67 91) or at the **Teatro Manzoni** (Via Manzoni 40, Tel: 79 05 43). Anyone keen on films can visit the following cinemas on the Corso Vittorio Emanuele (behind the Piazza del Duomo): **Corso**, **Astra**, **Excelsior**, **Mignon**, **Arlecchino**. The city's 'What's On' guide, called *La Notte*, will tell you what's being screened.

If you want to *fare bella figura*, elegant post-theatrical dining can be had at the **Ristorante Biffi Scala** (around 100,000 lire a head) or in cosier surroundings at the **Caffé Milano** (Piazza Mirabello 1, open till 3am, closed Sundays, good Irish coffee and delicious snacks, good value for money).

For dancing there's the **Nephentha** (Piazza Diaz 1, closed Sundays, not far from the Duomo), and for the gents, **Porta d'Oro** (Piazza Diaz 3, open till 4am, expensive strip-joint, 50,000 lire).

For those who just feel like a good glass of wine, **Al Ronchi** (Via S Maurillo 7, not far from the Duomo) stays open very late.

DAY 2

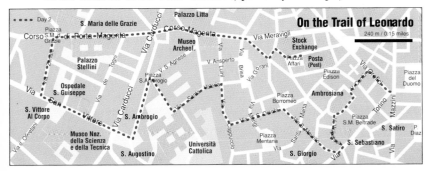

On the Trail of Leonardo da Vinci

From the Pinacoteca Ambrosiana to San Sepolcro, then to the Università Cattolica, the Museo della Scienza di Leonardo, S Maria delle Grazie, the Cenacolo di Leonardo and the Museo Archeologico.

San Sepolcro

– Tram 24 (Via Meravigli, Via Magenta);
Bus 50, 54 (S Ambrogio); Taxi 'Pinacoteca Ambrosiana' –

Today you'll be making the acquaintance of some famous names from Milanese history: the Borromeo cardinals, Leonardo da Vinci and St Ambrose. This itinerary begins at the Duomo once again, from where you should follow the Via Orefici as far as the Via Cantù, into which you turn left to arrive at the **Ambrosiana** (Piazza Pio XI, Tel: 800145, open daily except Saturday 9.30am–5pm, admission 3,000 lire). The **Biblioteca Ambrosiana** contains over 30,000 books including the world's oldest book of miniatures and also Leonardo da Vinci's *Codex Atlanticus*, which comprises over 1,000 pages of drawings and sketches by the universal genius. In the **Pinacoteca Ambrosiana** are works by Botticelli, Raphael, Titian and many other great painters – and in a glass case in Hall IV you'll find a lock of hair dyed blonde that once belonged to Lucrezia Borgia.

Leaving the Ambrosiana on the right-hand side via the Via Federico and passing several butcher's shops, you'll arrive at the **Piazza S Sepolcro**. Here, on the site of the former Roman forum, stands the church of S Sepolcro, consecrated to the holy sepulchre on the occasion of the First Crusade (open daily 8am–6pm). The

Romanesque crypt of this church contains a sarcophagus with reliquaries from the Holy Land dating from the High Middle Ages.

Opposite the church is a fine-looking Baroque building and a tower encased in cold, grey marble that Mussolini had added to the **Casa del Fascio** (1919) in 1939.

You can still find the original Milan in this area, with its narrow streets, craft workshops and elegant, patrician houses, most of them attractively restored. Off the beaten track and yet just a few steps from the Duomo, this is, however, one of the most expensive parts of the city (anyone buying property here has to expect a price equivalent to at least £5,000 per square metre). Walk down the Via Valpetrosa, then turn right down Via Torso and then right again straight away into the Via S Maurilio. At No 19 the wonderful courtyard of a 15th-century house awaits discovery – it is owned by the Crédit Agricole, Paris. In the Via S Marta you can admire the antique shops, and eat in the genuine atmosphere of the **Trattoria Milanese** for 30,000 or 40,000 lire: the *risotti* are excellent, especially if accompanied by a glass of *Barbera*.

Afterwards, one of the finest Rococo houses in Milan is located at No 3, Via Nerino, along with its magnificent courtyard and tiny roof-garden. Back in the Via S Maurilio once more, follow it as far as the **Piazza Borromeo**, which contains the *palazzo* of the same name. An old Padua family, the Borromeos had two particularly famous sons, the cardinals Federico and Carlo Borromeo, who were especially well-known for their charitable activities. Inside the *palazzo* is one of the most magnificent private courtyards in Milan.

Sometimes a friendly smile and a tip for the porter can open up finely-forged portals to reveal Milan's hidden treasures behind. Give this technique a try in the **Via Cappuccio**, where the *palazzo* at No 7 houses a magnificent kiosk dating from the 15th century.

Now go right and then left into the Via S Valeria, which emerges behind the Basilica di S Ambrogio into the *piazza* of the same name. On the left you'll see the entrance to the **Catholic University**, known in Milan as *La Cattolica*, one of the best in Italy. The university, one of four in Milan, and housed inside a former monastery, was founded in 1921 on the initiative of Padre Agostino Gemelli. On the other side of this large and leafy square you'll see the entrance to the finest Romanesque church in all Lombardy: **S Ambrogio**. It is in this building, far more than in the Duomo, that the Milanese are made most aware of their history; the church was founded as early as the 4th century, when St Ambrose, patron saint of Milan, arrived here from Trier in order to take up the post of governor. After having been elected Bishop, he placed himself at the head of the struggle against the Arian heretics. It was Ambrose who invented the style of church singing known as Ambrosian chant; he persuaded the Emperor Theodosius to accept Christianity as the state religion, and he also won over Augustine, the great philosopher and future father of the church, to the Christian faith.

The church, flanked by two towers, is entered through its atmospheric four-door portal. The interior, with three naves, is simple and almost severe. On the right-hand side at the very back, in the dome of the small apse, there are some 4th-century gold mosaics as well as a picture of St Ambrose. The man himself was buried in the church in AD397, and the urn containing his bones is in the crypt beneath the high altar. Above the altar is the vast *Ciborium*, a colourful gilded baldachin or canopy. The altar itself is completely covered with gold and silver containing around 400 precious stones – one of the most breathtaking pieces of religious art anywhere in the world. Ambrosian chant is still heard during the masses celebrated here.

Out in the square once more, note the pillar with the two holes in its base – they are supposed to have been put there by the horns of the devil.

The Festival of St Ambrose is celebrated every year on 7 December, and provides the cue for the *Fiera degli oh bei, oh bei* (a large fleamarket named after the calls of the stallholders) to begin on the Piazza. La Scala also begins its season on the same day. Anyone in Milan at this time should not miss paying a visit to this lively market. The children can fill themselves with *zucchero filato* (candy floss) or *calderoste* (hot chestnuts) while the grown-ups search for just the Christmas present they need at the various stalls.

Passing beneath the doors of the **Pusterla Gate** (which houses a remarkable museum of old weapons and instruments of torture) the itinerary now leaves the Piazza S Ambrogio and heads for the

S Ambrogio, mother of Milan's churches

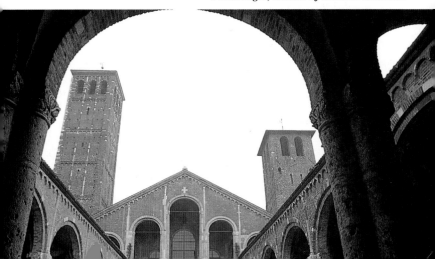

Leonardo da Vinci's 'The Last Supper'

Museo Nazionale della Scienza e della Tecnica di Leonardo da Vinci in the Via S Vittore (Tel: 463709, open daily except Monday 9.30am–4.50pm, admission 6,000 lire; you can find a detailed description of this collection in the 'Pick and Mix' section of this book under 'Museums, Museums, Museums').

Having admired Leonardo's scientific somersaults, it's now time for his artistic ones. Turning left on leaving the museum, and then right after 100 yards into the Via Zenale, you'll soon arrive in the Corso di Porta Magenta, and the *Cenacolo* (Refectory) of the church of **S Maria delle Grazie** (open daily except Monday 9am–1pm), where you can admire Leonardo's masterpiece *The Last Supper*. It's hard not to feel your heart beating just that little bit faster as you enter this former dining-hall of Dominican monks. The fresco began to deteriorate soon after it was finished, due to the dampness of the wall, and several of the subsequent attempts at restauration succeeded only in making matters worse. More skilful restauration techniques have been tried in recent years, but the condition of the fresco is still poor and its long-term survival remains in doubt. The painting, commissioned by Ludovico 'Il Moro' in 1495, displays several elements that were revolutionary at the time, for example the way the Apostles are depicted in realistically animated groups, with Judas included among them (fourth from the left). Miraculously, it survived an Allied bombing raid which almost completely destroyed the refectory which houses it in 1943. The church itself is the finest example of Early Renaissance architecture in Italy.

Continue along the Corso di Porta Magenta (anyone who feels like it can take a No 24 tram at this point to the Piazza Cordusio, where today's tour ends). After the junction with the Via Carducci you'll come face to face with the elegant **Palazzo Litta**, with its magnificent and typically Milanese golden-yellow Rococo facade. This *palazzo*, which was built by Ricchini, houses a fine little theatre at which I used to work many years ago. A short distance further on, at No 19, you could visit the **Museo Archeologico** (open daily except Monday 9.30am–noon and 3–6pm), but it might be a better idea to concentrate your remaining energies on the church of San Maurizio (open only on Wednesday, 9.30am–noon and 3–6pm, and on public holidays in summertime), with its fascinating frescoes by Bernardino Luini.

The Corso Magenta ends near San Maurizio, and the Via Meravigli begins; an excellent opportunity for a break. The **Bar Cavour** on the corner has a pleasant atmosphere, and an *aperitivo con stuzzichini* (aperitif with canapés) is just the thing. The building next door contains one of the oldest *drogherie* (grocer's shops) in Milan; here you can buy genuine *zafferano* (saffron), needed to create the famous *risotto giallo* ('yellow risotto'). See page 64 for the recipe.

The **Libreria Milanese**, on the left, contains everything that has ever been written about Milan. And since you're now nearby, why don't you take a quick look at the **Milan Stock Exchange** on the Piazza Affari? A close-up view of the trading floor can be had from the small visitors' gallery: there they all are, the elegant managers clad in their grey flannel suits, the soul of Milan! And now, at the Piazza Cordusio, today's itinerary has come to an end. I hope you enjoyed it.

After you've taken the time to rest a bit back at your hotel, how about a visit to Giorgio Strehler's **Piccolo Teatro** (Via Rovello 2, Tel: 877663, closed Monday)? We may even be performing a popular favourite, Carlo Goldoni's *Servant of Two Masters* for example. Or how about a film? Cinemas **Centrale 1 and 2** (Via Torino 30) are good, as are **De Amicis** (Via de Amicis 1) and the **Orchidea** (Via Terraggio 3a, not far from the Corso Magenta).

Or a literary coffee-house, perhaps? In the tiny **Caffé Portnoy** (Via de Amicis 1, open till 1am, closed Tuesday) you can spend an evening *à la Bohème* in the company of young poets and painters. You can even recite your own poetry and exhibit your own paintings here too – for free. Just consult the owner first.

Or there's always all-night Brazilian dancing at the **Sabor Tropical**, Via Cesare Correnti 12.

By way of contrast there's a relaxed and cosy atmosphere in the unpretentious and good-value **Osteria del Nuoto** (Via Ascanio Sforza 105, on the Naviglio Pavese, open till 3am): wine, beer, simple and delicious food – including excellent home-made desserts – shorten the night here.

The same goes for the **Osteria del Ballone** at Darsena del Naviglio/corner of Naviglio Grande, with excellent vegetarian dishes, delicious ice-creams and superb house wine (and there are also tables outside in the summer). And to round the day off, one more romantic stroll along the Naviglio Grande before retiring to bed.

What's on at the Piccolo Teatro

The Castello Sforzesco, former seat of power of the Visconti and Sforza families

DAY 3

Renaissance Splendour

A journey from medieval Milan around the Piazza Mercanti to the Via Dante and then on to the Renaissance highlights of the Castello Sforzesco and the Torre del Parco; then to the Brera quarter of the city for a Bohemian end to the day.

– Metro M2; Tram/Bus/Taxi 'Piazza Cordusio' –

The area between the Via Orefici and the Via Mercanti used to be the site of the *Comune di Milano*, or free city of Milan. The Middle Ages are still very much in evidence here, and on the **Piazza Mercanti**, former heart of the *Comune*, you can see the **Palazzo delle Ragione**, built in 1233, in which the City Council used to hold meetings until 1770. The magnificent **Loggia degli Osii** opposite, built in 1316, is however having to vie for attention with a fast food restaurant.

Leaving the square via the Via Mercanti, you'll immediately arrive at the **Piazza Cordusio**, a centre of business and a major traffic junction. There are banks everywhere here, the Stock Exchange isn't far away, and buses, taxis, trams and Metro trains all stop here. If you now let your eye travel up the amazingly straight Via Dante you can't miss the massive Castello Sforzesco at the other end. Before taking a closer look at that, however, I suggest you first turn off 50 yards further on into the Via Rovello, with the famous **Piccolo Teatro** at No 2.

Paolo Grassi and Giorgio Strehler founded Italy's first 'Teatro Stabile' here in 1947, and it later became world-famous. I always feel a bit nostalgic whenever I pass by this particular spot: the 10 years that I have spent in the dramaturgical department have had a marked effect on me.

Now go down a small street and return to the Via Dante, where you can enjoy an ice cream in the best *gelateria* in Milan (ice-cream shops are also referred to as *cremerie*). Further on, once you've arrived at the **Largo Cairoli**, with its Garibaldi equestrian statue, you'll have to pluck up some courage to cross the main traffic artery of the **Foro Buonaparte** in order to reach the Sforzas' castle. Napoleon, by the way, was crowned King of Italy in Milan's Duomo in 1805.

Assuming you're still in one piece once you've reached the other side of the street, you can now take a look at the **Castello Sforzesco**, the most important Renaissance structure in Milan. The castle was completely restored at the beginning of this century, and it was from here that the Viscontis and later the Sforzas ruled the city. The walls are 4m (13ft) thick, 31m (100ft) high and 200m (650ft) long; with its moats and drawbridges the castle, situated right in the middle of the city, was impregnable, and formed the power base for the two families' dictatorial regimes.

The castle is entered via the mighty, upward-tapering tower known as the **Torre Filarete**, a copy of the 15th-century original.

Then, once you've crossed the inner courtyard, the Cortile delle Milizie, and passed through one more gate, turn right towards the **Musei del Castello** (daily except Monday 9.30am–12.30pm and 2.30–5.30pm; more information on Milan's museums is contained in the 'Pick and Mix' section of this book under 'Museums, Museums, Museums'). The various collections in the Castello include paintings and sculpture but also arts, crafts and utensils. You can see a highlight in Hall 15: the not quite finished, magnificent *Pietà Rondanini* by Michelangelo, his last work before his death in 1564.

The Arco della Pace

The Porta del Barco, on the other side of the castle, gives access to the **Parco Sempione**, 42 hectares (103 acres) of parkland in which the **Arco della Pace**, built in the monumental Milanese style of the 19th century, was erected in honour of Napoleon in 1807.

Apart from this 'Arch of Peace', other sights include the **Palazzo dell'Arte**, with its fine art exhibitions, and the **Torre del Parco**, a tower over 100m (320ft) high, both constructed during the 1930s. Otherwise the park belongs to old people sitting on benches, groups of young people, or urban Indians practising their yoga. Unfortunately the park has to be patrolled by motorised *carabinieri* because it also seems to have become a popular battleground for skinheads and drug addicts. I suggest you only come here by day.

The painters Rino Sernaglia and Anna C

Having left the park along the Viale Gadio, where the tourist buses park, you'll pass by the **Acquario** (open daily except Monday 9am–12.30pm and 2–5pm). This aquarium contains 48 pools with all manner of fish, reptiles and amphibians, and is a huge favourite with the city's schoolchildren.

If you now continue along the Foro Buonaparte for a while, you'll soon find yourself in front of the new home of the Piccolo Teatro, which has been under construction for years. The Via Tivoli leads to the Via Mercato and Milan's Brera gallery area; many of the city's artists live in the courtyards of the simple houses here. (One inspiration amongst them is Anna Canali, who runs the **Arte Struktura** gallery on the second floor of Via Mercato 1. Anna is the heart and soul of the group of artists known as Madi which includes such famous names as Rino Sernaglia, Salvator Presta and Dupré: the group is distinctive for its cinematographic, three-dimensional style.)

Art in Milan has a long tradition. The Romantic *scapigliati* artists of the last century (so named because they did not wear the tall hats fashionable at that time) turned the **Brera Quarter** into a real den of Bohemianism. In the Via Pontaccio, the extension of the Via Tivoli and the Via Fiori Chiari, there are rows of galleries and – as the Milanese call them – 'neoliberty' restaurants, where the patrons are

Via Fiori Chiari

very 'in' and very 'arty'. On the corner of the Via Solferino, Italy's important daily newspaper, the *Corriere della Sera*, provides political and intellectual fodder for those with Bohemian lifestyles in the Brera, many of them students from the Accademia delle Belle Arti, housed in the **Palazzo Brera** on the Via Fiori Oscuri. Originally built in the 16th century for the Jesuits according to plans by Ricchini, the Palazzo also contains one of the most famous collections of paintings in the world: the **Pinacoteca di Brera** (open Tuesday to Saturday 9am–2pm, Sunday 9am–1pm; rumour has it that all-day opening from 1993 onwards is being considered).

In the Brera Quarter you can also visit the famous **Biblioteca Braidense**, the **Osservatorio Astronomico** and the **Orto Botanico** (all three of them are situated in the Palazzo Brera, Via Brera 28).

After such a *tour de force* you'll definitely be in need of some refreshment, which can be found at the already legendary **Bar Giamaica** (Via Brera 32), a home from home for generations of painters, writers and musicians.

And this evening? *Che facchiamo stasera?* Why not visit the **Nuovo Piccolo Teatro**, Via Rivoli 6 (Metro M1, get out at 'Lanzi'), where there's always a host of European avantgarde productions.

Cena dopo teatro? You can stay in the area for your post-theatrical supper, and try out one of the many Chinese or Vietnamese restaurants in Milan's 'Chinatown': the restaurants in the Via Paolo Sarpi on the northern side of the Parco

Entrance to Castello Sforzesco

are cheap (30,000 lire a head) and usually stay open until 4am. If you didn't visit the above-mentioned Bar Giamaica this afternoon, you could always take a look at it this evening: half bar and half restaurant, this establishment is very lively and has imaginative dishes (main courses at 20,000 lire) and cocktails created by the

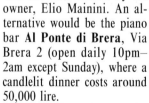

owner, Elio Mainini. An alternative would be the piano bar **Al Ponte di Brera**, Via Brera 2 (open daily 10pm–2am except Sunday), where a candlelit dinner costs around 50,000 lire.

Volete ballare? Anyone who still feels energetic can head for the discotheque called **Rolling Stone**, Corso XXII Marzo 32 (a pretty wild place, and only really for young people).

1. In Search of Lost Milan

A short discovery trip into remote medieval corners around the Piazza Torino and Roman Milan: from the gourmet temple Peck to S Satiro, S Lorenzo and the Porta Ticinese, then on to the Corsa Porta Ticinese, S Eustorgio and the Piazza XXIV Maggio.

The following 'Pick and Mix' section provides itineraries that reveal several different aspects of Milan. As an interested observer, the visitor can experience the city close up, beyond the familiar sights and views, or he can follow his own personal inclinations.

– Metro M2; Tram, Bus, Taxi 'Piazza Cordusio' –

This itinerary begins at the Duomo, which can be reached by taking the Via Orefici from the Piazza Cordusio. The first stop is in the Via Torino, but even before beginning the route something may already tempt you to take a break: just after the Via Spadari there's the enticing gourmet temple **Peck**, with its superb aromas and specialities; step into the *rosticceria*, take a look around and try a few things out! On the right are the *antipasti* with their delicious sauces, superbly arranged lobster, delicious smoked salmon and seafood. Ahead of you there's the cheese, the meat, the salami and the *pasta* – all of it super-expensive, naturally.

Outside in the Via Spadari are more delicatessens belonging to the Peck family, such as the fishmongers and also the *Bottega del maiale*, the pork butcher's. In the nearby Via Hugo Peck also own the *rosticceria* and *enoteca* **Scoffone**,

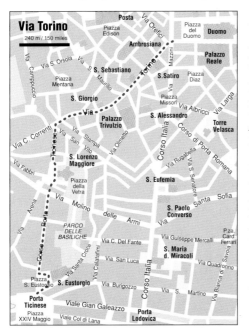

where you can have a quick aperitif and a small snack.

Enough of all this food, though – it's time for some culture!

Back in the Via Torino, drop in on St Ambrose's brother: his church, **S Satiro**, was built in 1478 by Bramante, incorporating the former smaller Carolingian church. Don't miss the slender, magnificent baptistry on the right-hand side.

Return to the Via Torino and follow the street as far as **S Giorgio al Palazzo**, a Rococo church, its interior adorned by *Scenes from the Passion of Christ*, a magnificent cycle of paintings by Luini. The **Via Nerino** starts on the left-hand side of the church. In this street it's worth winning over some more grumpy-looking doorkeepers outside the medieval *palazzi* with a cheery smile and the odd bit of cash, because there are some breathtaking gardens to be seen behind the gates. Also worthy of note in this respect are the Via San Maurilio (with its craft shops) and the Via S Marta.

After this diversion, continue along the Via Torino as far as the **Carrobio** (from the Latin word *quadrivium*, meaning road junction) where, keeping to the left-hand side of the street, you bear left and turn into the **Corso Porta Ticinese**, with the true highlight of today's tour: the **Colonne Romane di San Lorenzo**. The Roman columns of S Lorenzo represent a magnificent period of the Roman and Early Christian history of Milan. Once part of a pagan temple, the

Roman columns and the Basilica San Lorenzo

columns were erected in the 4th century in the form of a triumphal entry arch in front of S Lorenzo – at a time when Milan was still the capital of the Western Roman Empire and the Emperor Constantine's Edict of Milan, which granted the Christians freedom of belief, had only just been passed. Times certainly do change.

In front of this, Milan's oldest basilica, which was probably Arian once before it was catholicised, stands a statue in memory of Constantine (the original stands in the courtyard of S Giovanni in Laterano in Rome), whose conversion in the year 312 led to the rise of Christianity as a world religion. Inside the basilica, the **Chapel of S Aquilino**, on the right, is worthy of particular note. St Aquilinus came from Würzburg and was killed in the 4th century during the religious struggles between the Arians and the Catholics (the doctrine of Arius affirmed the created, finite nature of Christ). There are some magnificent 5th-century mosaics and frescoes in the octagonal chapel.

Having left S Lorenzo, you should take a swift look at the **Porta Ticinese**, one of the city's two surviving medieval gates. Rather than going through it, however, you should now make for the

Parco delle Basiliche behind San Lorenzo (beyond the Via Mulino delle Armi). Stroll along narrow, leafy paths, past mothers, baby-sitters, old people, children and dogs in a southerly direction until you reach the apse and the Romanesque church tower of the **Basilica di S Eustorgio**. The interior doesn't live

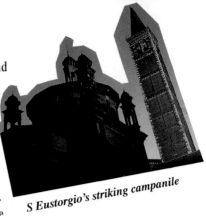

S Eustorgio's striking campanile

up to the magnificent facade by any means. The reliquaries of the Three Magi were kept here in the **Capella dei Magi** from the 4th century onwards until Barbarossa took them to Cologne. Part of the reliquary was returned recently, and since then, on 6 January, during *Epifania* (Epiphany), a procession – complete with camels – leads from S Eustorgio to the Duomo. The **Capella Portinari** needs a mention, too: it's one of the finest pieces of Renaissance architecture in all Milan, with frescos by Vincenzo Foppa.

Today's itinerary ends at the mighty **Arco della Pace**, on the Piazza XXIV Maggio.

2. Around the Navigli by Bus

A round trip along the filled-in 'navigli'. Take the 97 bus (or the 96 bus going the other way) from the Piazza Cadorna via Pusterla di S Ambrogio, S Maria presso S Celso, Basilica di S Nazaro, Università Statale, Palazzo Sormani and Corso Monforte to the Galleria d'Arte Moderna. Best done in the afternoon.

– Metro M1 Piazza Cadorna; Taxi 'Piazza Cadorna' –

Did you know that Milan was once a city of canals? That the city was filled with a whole series of them, mostly man-made, connecting it with the lakes to the north and the Po and Ticino rivers? That a system of sluices dating back to medieval times (Leonardo himself is said to have had a hand in their design) allowed ships to travel right into the heart of Milan? *Navigli* was the name given to these canals. The Milan so beloved of Heine and Stendhal contained a great deal more water than it does today.

During Emperor Barbarossa's time, the *navigli* were still defensive trenches that had been dug around the medieval city. In the 16th century they developed into important transport routes, and craftsmen, merchants and noblemen settled along them – just as they did along the Canale Grande in Venice. At the end of the last century the costs involved in their upkeep increased to such an extent that the *navigli* began to be filled in. The real *coup de grâce*, however, was delivered in the 1930s by the public transport system, which needed a great deal of space.

So just close your eyes and imagine for a moment that your bus is actually being 'rowed' around the city! The route begins *'alla Nord'* (at the **north station**) – or in the Piazza Cadorna if you've arrived on the M1 Metro line – where to the left of the station, bus No 97 leaves from the Via Minghetti. The route leads along the Via Carducci, past the Pusterla di S Ambrogio and through the Via De Amicis, both of which once formed part of the inner *naviglio*. Alight after the Porta Ticinese at the **Parco delle Basiliche**.

In the Via Mulino delle Armi you could pay a quick visit to Guilia Cerronceva at No 7; her shop, **Il Gioiello di Pietra**, is a real treasure trove for those interested in fossils and minerals. You could also take a look at the church of **S Maria presso S Celso** to the right. A statue of the Madonna which is supposed to work miracles, situated next to the main altar here, is a popular destination for many Milanese newly-weds.

The journey continues on the 97 bus again, along the Via Santa Sofia, and alights two stops further on at the junction with the Corsa di Porta Romana. Keeping to the left, a few steps further on you'll find yourself standing on the small square dominated by the **Basilica di S Nazaro**, which dates from the time of St Ambrose.

Behind the basilica, follow the small street that leads to the Largo Richetti and the famous **Università Statale**, also referred to as *Cà Grande*, within its 15th-century walls. Inside the magnificent courtyard of the university, with its grandiose-looking Loggia, you can eat a sandwich and mix with the students, or take the Via Festa del Perdono back to the *naviglio*, which here is buried beneath the asphalt of the **Via Francesco Sforza** (named after the university's founder). Following this street as far as its junction with the Corso di Porta Vittoria, you'll come to the magnificent **Palazzo Sormani**. This glorious Rococo building once stood on the bank of the *naviglio*, and today it houses the **Biblioteca Civica**. This well-stocked library also boasts an extensive collection of works by Stendhal.

Students from the Università Statale

Now cross the Corso and continue straight on until you arrive in the Via Visconti di Modrone. Stop here! It is time for a break in the **Taveggia** *pasticceria*, where lawyers from the nearby Palace of Justice go to gain strength between sittings; try the famous *budini di riso* (rice pudding), the delicious *babà* (biscuits) and the ever-fresh *meringhe* (meringues). By the way, the great Italian writer Alessandro Manzoni was born in No 17 Via Visconti di Modrone.

Back aboard the No 97 bus, get

off two stops further on at the Corso Monforte. In the first street on the left, the Via Conservatorio, is the **Conservatorio**, founded in 1807 by Eugenio de Beauharnais, where both Puccini and Victor de Sabata once studied. Then comes the second-largest church in all Milan, **S Maria della Passione**, towering above the corner of the Via Bellini. The building was begun in the 16th century, and it contains Gaudenzio Ferrari's masterpiece, *Ultima Cena*. The chapter house, filled with frescoes, is also very impressive.

Back now to the Corso Monforte, where I suggest you take the bus once more and get off in the **Piazza Cavour**. From here, along-side the tall Palazzo dei Giornali, the bamboo-lined Via Palestro leads to the orange facade of the **Villa Reale**, housing the **Galleria d'Arte Moderna** (open daily except Tuesday 9.30am–noon, 2.30–5.30pm). This neoclassical building, designed by the Viennese architect Pollock, in which Napoleon once resided, has 35 exhibition halls full of 19th- and 20th-century painting and sculpture.

But now it's time for a good lunch or supper. How about **Leonardo's**, Via Senato 43, where you can end this tour *in bellezza* dining on *carpaccio, bresaole* and *filetti*.

3. Milan's Amsterdam

Walks (in the daytime) and entertainment (at night) along the 'navigli' canals at the Porta Ticinese. From the Piazza XXIV Maggio via the Darsena to the Naviglio Grande, the Naviglio Pavese and the Corso San Gottardo.

– Tram No 15 from the Duomo to the Piazza XXIV Maggio –

This route should really be done twice: by day in order to discover popular, everyday Milan, and then once again in the evening when the Milan 'scene' is in full swing – around the *navigli* is where Milan lets its hair down, and indulges in eating, drinking and dancing.

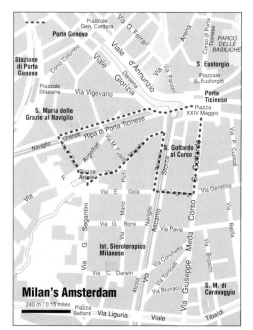

Milan's Amsterdam

240 m / 0.15 miles

It's hard to imagine to-day, but as recently as the 1970s Milan had the third largest port in all of Italy in terms of tonnage, and barges carrying sand and gravel used to travel into the city along the *navigli*. Those days are gone now, but a look at the canals which survive is still very worthwhile.

Go up from the Piazza XXIV Maggio to the **Darsena** (the former harbour basin), having taken a quick look at the lively and picturesque **Mercato Comunale** on the way. The best view of the *navigli* and the old houses along their banks can be had from the green kiosk. On the other side of the Darsena the Fiera di Sinigallia, a kind of flea market, is held every Saturday.

Down at the **Naviglio Grande**, all of Milan meets up on the last Sunday in every month to stroll around the **Mercatone dell'Antiquariato**. You can find objects of all shapes and sizes on the many stalls here, some old, some not so old,

Sinigallia flea market

and several of them priced astronomically high – but the atmosphere of the place is unique.

Walking along the right bank of the Naviglio Grande and after 100 yards or so you'll come across the remains of the **Vicolo dei Lavandai**, the old wash-houses that used to line the bank of the *naviglio* in former days. The steps and stone slabs on which the women of the quarter used to wash their clothing – without detergent – can still be seen on the bank here. The Vicolo also contains the **El Brellin'** restaurant, by the way, which stays open late and serves excellent Lombard cuisine.

Beyond the late 19th-century church of **S Maria delle Grazie** you can stand on the small bridge above the canal and observe all the small shops, art galleries and *pizzerie* along the bank. Just imagine, this artificial waterway was built in the 14th century, and it leads in a straight line all the way to the Ticino river, more than 50km (30 miles) away! If you were to turn right here and carry straight on you'd reach the **Stazione di Porta Genova**, a colourful quarter of the city, with a bookshop in the Via Vigevano that deals exclusively with Celtic literature.

For the time being however, leave the bridge on the left bank of the canal, the Ripa di Porta Ticinese, and turn immediately into the Via Paoli, which you should follow as far as the **Piazza Arcole**. This is one of the rare areas of green in the quarter, and in the summer you can swim in the **Piscina Argelati**. Unfortunately even this green area is due to be built over soon. Now turn left and enter the **Via Magolfa** where one of the city's remaining *osterie* with good *Barbera* wine, salami, sausages and sometimes even roast frog continues to keep the spirit of old Milanese hospitality alive.

The Via Magolfa opens out into the **Naviglio Pavese**, where the drinks are on me – after all, I live here! How about an aperitif mixed by my friend Carlo in the bar 100 yards further on, on the right-hand side of the street? Or a *panino con birra* in the **Birreria** at the beginning of the *naviglio*? By the way, note the large number of houseboats in the *naviglio*.

After a drink at Carlo's place you can cross the canal – no, a Canale Grande it definitely isn't, but it's still a canal despite that: 33km (20 miles) long, and built by the Viscontis. Over 1,400 barges used to travel along it each year! Following the Via Ascanio Sforza on the other side, you should sample the delicious, home-made pasta and risotto sauces at **Wilma e Riccardo** at No 17. At No 15 go through a connecting courtyard, with its fine old houses and balconies, and emerge on the other side in the Corso San Gottardo. Worthy of note here, alongside the huge variety of shops, is the intimate little church of **S Gottardo al Corso** at No 6, with its modern windows by Aldo Carpi. And now you're back in the Piazza XXIV Maggio again, where you can take a No 15 tram back to the Duomo.

Anyone who has a car with them should use it to visit the **Chiesa di S Cristoforo sul Naviglio** (ten minutes by car along the Naviglio Grande as far as Via S Cristoforo). Ludivico il Moro and Beatrice d'Este were married here, and this exquisite church is still very popular indeed with Milan's prospective newly-weds.

And in the evening? *Follie!!* After 10pm the bars along the *navigli* are invaded, mostly by young people from the city centre and the drearier suburbs, all of them eager for a good time. In summer they sit along the banks and eat icecream, or patronize the houseboat-pizzerias **Alla Pesa** or **Scimmie**. This is the place to hang out.

The navigli district by night

4. Around the City Walls

A trip along Milan's historic city limits on a No 29 tram (returning on a No 30). From the Piazza Missori to the Via degli Amadei, the Porta Romana, the Porta Venezia, the Giardini Pubblici with the Museo Scienze Naturali, and then on to the Piazza della Repubblica. Best done in the afternoon.

– Metro M1, station Duomo;
Taxi 'Piazza Missori' –

From the Duomo it's only 200 yards' walk south to reach the **Piazza Missori**, where today's discovery trip begins. On the way to the Corso Italia on

the Piazza Bertarelli, I suggest you take a small detour along the **Via degli Amadei**, one of the few streets in Milan to have retained its historic character – notice the beautiful inner courtyards as well as the excellent seafood restaurant **L'Assassino** (closed Tuesday).

Palazzo della Giustizia

On the Piazza Bertarelli, with the magnificent palace housing the **Touring Club** (tourist information is also available here), hop on a No 56 bus as far as the Porta Ludovica. Continue on to the Via Col di Lana, where you can catch a No 29 tram for five stops to the Piazzale Medaglie d'Oro. Now you've reached the **Porta Romana**, erected in honour of the marriage of the Austrian archduchess Margaret to Philip III of Spain in 1599 (when Milan was Spanish). The gate once formed part of the Spanish walls, which extended for a distance of 11km (7 miles) around the city. To the left of the Porta Romana runs the Corso of the same name, a lively boulevard with theatres and cabarets.

Take another 29 tram now and travel four stops on it to the **Porta Vittoria** in the Piazzale Cinque Giornati, so named because of the five-day-long rebellion in 1848 against Austrian rule. At the end of the Corso di Porta Vittoria, on the left hand side, you can't fail to see the colossal, almost Kafkaesque **Palazzo della Giustizia**, built in 1935. It's a real experience just wandering through the enormous halls inside this building; it makes you feel very small and very lost.

Mustn't get distracted, though! So take another No 29 tram now in the direction of the Stazione Centrale; after two stops it reaches the Piazza Tricolore, and then two stops further on, the **Porta Venezia**. Just a few steps now in the direction of Corso di Porta Venezia is the entrance to the **Giardini Pubblici**. Laid out in Italian style with English elements, this park, 17ha (42 acres) in size, contains a 600-seat **Planetarium** founded in 1930 by Ulrich Hoepli, a Swiss editor of scientific books (open from 9pm Tuesday and Thursday, and 3–4.30pm on Saturday and Sunday) and also the **Civico Museo di Storia Naturale**. The latter contains over a million insects, 100,000 fossils, 24,000 stuffed birds, 17,000 mineral specimens as well as an extensive library (open daily except Monday 9.30am–12.30pm, 2–5pm, November to February 9.30am–12.30pm, 2.30–5.30pm).

Now you can get back by tram No 29 at the Porta Venezia, and continue in the direction of the Stazione Centrale for another two stops before saying a final farewell to the city's tram system at the **Piazza della Repubblica**. At the beginning of the Via Turati you'll notice twin towers dating from the 1960s, while from the direction of the broad Via Vettor Pisani the Pirelli building, Milan's first ever skyscraper, comes into view. The square also contains several luxury hotels, such as the Jolly Hotel Touring.

Anyone feeling tired at this point can take the M3 back to the Duomo, otherwise it's onward, down the Via Turati, as far as the Piazza Cavour. On the way is the **Palazzo della Permanente**, an exhibition building, and in the Via Moscova the church of S **Angelo** and the famous **Angelicum Cultural Centre**. This itinerary finishes at the Piazza Cavour, and with a calm conscience you can now take the M3 back to the Duomo, and go over to the Galleria for an aperitif at the **Camparino**.

Outside a Milan gallery

5. The Art of Milan

A highly condensed tour of art galleries and antique shops.

– Metro M1 and then on foot –

Got your city map? And your cheque book? And are your shoelaces tied? Good. On this trip you may be provided with an (aesthetic) offer you can't refuse: everything gets sold in Milan, and sometimes there are some really excellent bargains to be had.

As always, the tour begins at the Duomo, from where you take the M1 to the stop **Palestro**. From here it's up to you!

Bergamini, Corso Venezia 16: an old-established gallery, 19th-century masters, the first Masson exhibition in Italy.

Antichità Venezia, Corso Venezia 6: fine 18th-century paintings.

Galleria Blu, Via Senato 18: founded 1957, international experimentalists eg Kandinsky, Klee, Léger, Turcato, Santomaso.

At this point you'll need to check the city map again so as not to lose your bearings:

Lorenzelli, Via Sant'Andrea 19: international classical abstracts eg Magnelli, Licini, Poliakoff, large warehouse.

Agrifoglio, Via Montenapoleone 21: design and fashion.

Daverio, Via Montenapoleone 6: De Chirico, Sironi, Savinio, Depero, Trans avantgarde.

Arte Antica, Via Sant'Andrea 11: Pasquale Falanga has 18th-century French and Italian furniture, Italian, European and Chinese porcelain as well as Italian and German silver.

On now to the Via Gesù, doubtless the most renowned (ie 'in') gallery street of Milan:

Studio 111, Via Gesù 7: Vittoria Marinetti, daughter of the founder of Futurism, puts on select exhibitions featuring painters such as the Aerofuturist Tullio Crali.

Gilli, Via Gesù 17: a small salon, exhibitions of old art, especially 16th-century drawings and
sketches; with luck you can find
rare works by Tiepolo, Guercino
or Luca Giordano. The gallery
Stanza del Borgo, Via Puccini 5, is
its opposite number.

Gian Ferrari, Via Gesù 19: one of
the best-known galleries in Milan,
founded in 1936, run by Claudia Ferrari who, like her father before her, is
an art critic and an expert on 20th-
century art; Sironi, Casorati, Martini,
De Pisis, Pirandello, Rossi, etc. Large,
richly-stocked warehouse and archive,
with access allowed.

A gallery owner and his art

You've now reached the **Via Manzoni**, the cultural watershed between the area around the Via Montenapoleone (Milan's *rive droite*) and the Brera (its *rive gauche*).

Naviglio, Via Manzoni 45, belongs to the Cardazzo brothers, with brother Renato running the gallery; they were the pioneers of the international avantgarde in Italy, and have another gallery in Venice. They were the first to introduce Pollock, Calder and Fontana to Italy.

Centro Annunciata, Via Manzoni 44: 20th-century painters up to Picasso and the Surrealist masters.

Milione, Via Bigli 19: a side-street off the Via Manzoni, old-established gallery that introduced Léger and Kandinsky; various attractions ranging from Fellini sketches to Magritte.

Now it's time to take a look at the *rive gauche*, the **Brera**. After taking the Via Verdi past the Scala, follow the Via Brera, which was the centre of the gallery scene until the arrival of banks and financial holdings resulted in astronomic increases in rents.

Arte Centro, Via Brera 11: classic abstracts by Prampolini,

Cioni, Jiro Sugewana.

Il Diaframma, Via Brera 16: experimental photography.

Galleria 32, Via Brera 6: realists and social realists such as José Ortega and Alfred Hrdlika, erotic graphics by Picasso.

On the Piazza del Carmine not far from the Brera there are two more famous galleries:

Compagnia del Disegno, Via del Carmine 11: Alain Toubas and his friends have a collection of contemporary art here including work by Crocchi, Daminao and Keimitzuchi.

This beautiful little square with its cobblestones also contains the Lombard Neo-Gothic church of **S Maria del Carmine** (containing fine paintings by Procaccini) and alongside it, next to a shop that sells delicious cakes and jams (excuse this brief digression), is the **Braidense** gallery belonging to Paolo Pocchini, one of the most daring and hard-working gallery-owners in Milan.

Now you'll probably have had just about enough. Of course, Milan does have an enormous number of art galleries, and anyone who isn't too tired can try the following (not on this tour, though):

Gastaldelli, Piazza Castello 22 (not far from the Castello Sforzesco): an Italian potpourri with Dorati, Scanavino, Sernaglia, Arroyo, Matta, Masson, Rainer, Tapiés.

Grossetti, Via dei Piatti 9: spacious interior, painters such as Spagnulo, Manzoni, Kolibal and also various young hopefuls.

Yes, but what about the antiques, you may be asking! They're scattered all over the city, but I recommend the area between the Via Torino, the Via S Maurilio and the Via Santa Marta, and also the vicinity of the Porta Ticinese. Here are a few names:

Al Piccolo Naviglio, Naviglio Grande 34: 'freestyle' objects and lots of mirrors.

Cazzaniga, Via Lanzone 1: art from the 15th to the 19th century, old ivory.

Della Francesca,
'Madonna del Duca Federico'

Silvia Blanchaert, Via Nirone 19: very attractive shop with magnificent lamps (Murano glass by Venini) from the 1930s.

Nella Longari, Via Bigli 15: rare and very valuable pieces.

To finish off, just a reminder of where to find the antique markets:

Oh bei, Oh bei on 7 December in front of S Ambrogio, **Fiera di Sinigalla** every Saturday on the Darsena del Naviglio (very popular with all architects and interior designers), **Mercatino di Brera**, every third Saturday in the month, and the **Mercatino dell'Antiquariato** along the *navigli* on every last Sunday in the month.

44

```
          THE CIVILIZED TRAVELLER
               2003 BROADWAY
           NEW YORK NYC 10023
               212-875-0306
           Transaction No: 20695
  10/01/93  11:41:33    CLERK:ANTHO


   1 @   9.95 0395657660      $    9.95
              INSIGHT POCKET


  SUBTOTAL                    $    9.95
  TAX @ 8.250%                $    0.82
  TOTAL                       $   10.77
  CASH                        $   15.00
  TOTAL PAID                  $   15.00
  CHANGE                      $    4.23


              THANK YOU!
     'BON VOYAGE'     NO BOOK EXCHANGES

MERCH EXCHGE OR STORE CR ONLY IN 7 DAYS
```

6. Museums, Museums, Museums

A round-up of the best.

This selection really needs to be organised according to what you're interested in. You've already seen a few of Milan's 50 or more museums, and here is a more detailed summary. Each museum has useful catalogues; most are closed on Monday.

In the city of Leonardo, the first museum on the list is of course the **Museo Nazionale della Scienza e della Tecnica**: Via S Vittore 19/21 (open daily except Monday 9.30am–4.50pm; Metro M2 or bus Nos 50, 54, 96, 97; admission free). In the *Galleria di Leonardo* models based on Leonardo's original sketches can be seen. There are also sections on aviation, transport, electricity, industrial machinery, motors, computer science, etc. The **Museo Navale Didattico** in the building next door has an interesting display of model ships.

Raffaello Sanzio: 'Betrothal of the Virgin'

The **Musei del Castello Sforzesco** are justly renowned (open daily except Monday 9.30am–12.30pm, 2.40–5.15pm; Metro M1/2; admission free). Antique arts and crafts: Michelangelo's *Pietà Rondanini* is in Hall 15; in Hall 3 there is the imposing equestrian statue of *Bernabò Visconti di Bonino*; the **picture gallery** contains works by Tintoretto, Mantegna, Bellini and Lotto; the **Bertarelli stamp collection** has over a million exhibits, some of them priceless; the **archaeological and numismatic collection** contains prehistoric, Egyptian and other finds; and the **arts and crafts collection** has furniture, wall-hangings and ceramics.

Galleria d'Arte Moderna, Via Palestro 16 (open daily except Tuesday 9.30am–12.30pm, 2.30–5.30pm; Metro M1, get off at Palestro; admission free). Italian and European painters, Futurists, Marino Marini Museum, French Impressionists, Renoir, Van Gogh, Cézanne, many exhibitions.

Pinacoteca di Brera, Via Brera 28 (open Monday to Saturday 9am–1.30pm, Sunday 9am–12.30pm; bus No 43; tram Nos 1, 4, 8, 12 Piazza della Scala; admission). Because of a long-drawn-out argument between museum attendants and the museum administration about the *'ora d'aria'*, the above opening times may not be reliable. The attendants want one (paid) hour outside in the 'fresh air' daily and the museum administration doesn't agree. The Pinacoteca, along with the Uffizi in Florence, is among the most important museums in the world and includes works by della Francesca, Raphael, Caravaggio, Titian and Bellini.

Museo Poldi Pezzoli, Via Morone 8 (open Thursday to Sunday 9.30am–12.30pm, 2.30–7.30pm; Tuesday and Wednesday 9.30am–12.30pm, 2–6pm; the museum is two minutes' walk from the Piazza della Scala; admission). Botticelli; a wonderful picture by Pollaiolo, the 15th-century *Ritratto di giovane donna* (profile of a young woman); tapestries, hangings, clocks, weapons and more.

Museo Archeologico, Corso Magenta 15 (open daily except Tuesday 9.30am–12.30pm, 2.30–5.30pm; bus Nos 50, 54, 96, 97; tram Nos 19, 24; admission free). Also interesting for Milanese history, with an impressive model of Roman Milan; also Prehistoric, Etruscan, Egyptian collections, etc.

Pinacoteca Ambrosiana, Piazza Pio XI, not far from the Duomo (open daily except Saturday 9.30am–5pm; admission). Founded by Federico Borromeo. Botticelli, Raphael, Titian and Caravaggio's grandiose *Canestro di Frutta*.

Alfa Romeo and Milan share the same coat of arms

Museo Storico Alfa Romeo in Arese (open daily except Saturday 9am–noon, 2.30–4.30pm; admission free on public holidays; Tel: 93392303). See the legendary prototypes driven by Nuvolari, Farina and Fangio (1950–55), and also Niki Lauda's Brabham Alfa (1979).

Museo Teatrale alla Scala, Piazza della Scala (open daily 9am–noon, 2–6pm October to April; closed Sunday; admission). Musical instruments, scores, letters, photographs of operatic luminaries and sculptures etc. A superb documentation of La Scala up to the present day.

Museo del Giocattolo e del Bambino, Ripa Ticinese 27 (open daily except Monday 9.30am–12.30pm, 3–7pm; tram Nos 9, 29, 15, 30, Piazza XXIV Maggio). Fascinating collection of toys throughout the ages.

7. The Fashion World

A walk through the city's fashion quarter and its pedestrian precinct. From the Piazza del Duomo to the Corso Vittorio Emanuele, S Fidele, the Via Manzoni, the Via Montenapoleone, the Piazza Babila and the Via Durini to the Largo Augusto.

Today is definitely the day to *fare una bella figura*. Today you can kit yourself out at Armani or Mila Schön, put on some Ferragamo shoes, stick a Vuitton handbag under your arm and complete the entire outfit with a few pieces of Renaissance jewellery by Buccellati; for today you're off to the fashion sanctuary known as the *'quadrilatero',* where the ultimate in luxury can be admired – and even bought. Do allow me, though, to point out the odd sight along the way too.

After visiting the Milanese super-boutique **La Rinascente** (which by the way has a superb view of the Duomo, from the café terrace on the 7th floor) you can start off at the top of the **Corso Vittorio Emanuele** and turn left across the Via S Paolo and the Via Hoepli to reach the magnificent **Chiesa di S Fidele**. Built by the Jesuits in the 16th century, this is the equivalent of the Madeleine in Paris, and the temple of the Milanese aristocracy (magnificent choir stalls, exquisite confessional).

From here the route follows the Via Omoni as far as the **Piazza Belgioioso**. On the corner of the Via Moroni is a small brick *palazzo*, once the home of Alessandro Manzoni, Italy's greatest 19th-century author.

The **Museo Manzoni** inside (open Tuesday to Friday 9am–noon, 2–4pm) contains several of Manzoni's documents and personal requisites. The **Via Manzoni**, one of the busiest streets in the city, leads off the square. Neoclassical *palazzi* such as the **Palazzo Borromeo d'Adda** (No 39–41), where Stendhal once resided, and also the **Hôtel Milan** where Giuseppe Verdi lived and died, give the Via Manzoni its authentic *carattere ottocentesco*. Just a little further on is one of Milan's finest streets, the **Via Bigli** (the poet Montale once lived in the **Palazzo Bigli-Ponti** at No 11; its inner courtyard contains several fine 16th-century frescoes).

The **Via Montenapoleone** is the backbone of all the other fashion streets of S Spirito, Borgospesso, Gesù, S Andrea and della Spiga.

Fashion's shop-window

The *'Montenapo',* as it is familiarly called, does of course contain such great names as Missoni, Ferragamo, Gucci, etc. but here you will also find such shops as Lorenzi (knives large and small), Venini (Murano glass) and Jesurum (Venetian lace). The *palazzo* with the magnificent inner courtyard in the Via Gesù belongs to Gianni Versace. Back in the Via della Spiga it's *alta moda* again: the Versace shop at No 4, Ferré at No 12, and Krizia at No 23. By way of contrast Subert, at No 22, sells old scientific instruments.

Situated in the Via S Andrea, the **Palazzo Morando** at No 6 contains the fascinating **Museo di Milano** (open

Buon appetito!

9.30am–12.15pm, 2.30–5.15pm). Museum administrator Dr. Anna Mangano has collected together an absolute wealth of historical material. Also in the Via S Andrea are Armani (No 9), Lange (No 11), and Luciano Soprani (No 14). Now continue on in the direction of the *Montenapo* but just before reaching it, turn left into the Via Bagutta. Here, in the famous **Ristorante Bagutta**, the most important prizes in the Italian literary world are handed out each year. Many photographs of famous artists adorn the walls, and the food is excellent too. The Via Bagutta emerges into the Piazza S Babila, which you now cross in order to enter the **Via Durini**. Here you'll see some magnificent baroque *palazzi* dating from the Spanish period, especially the huge **Palazzo Durini** at No 24. Arturo Toscanini, the famous conductor, used to live at No 20.

The Via Durini leads into the Largo Augusto, from where the Via Verziere (once a fruit and vegetable market) runs towards the **Piazza S Stefano** and the huge Romanesque basilica of the same name, which contains a fine fresco by Sebastiano Ricci.

If you're hungry at the end of this itinerary, the picturesque townhouses around the Piazza contain a lot of unpretentious and very pleasant small restaurants frequented by students from the nearby Università Statale: **Margy Burger** (No 2, *panini, tavola calda, salsicce*, 10pm–3am); **Lo Stregone** (No 8, home-made ice cream, beer); **Pizza Pazza** (No 10, every conceivable type of pizza, also other starters and main courses); **Pane e Focaccia** (No 10, pizza slices, *panzerotti*); **Rosticceria** (No 10, very good *tavola calda*, try the stuffed mushrooms); and **Vino e Olio** (No 12, delicious specialities, *ghiotonnerie*).

8. From the Central Station to S Siro

A look at a few of Milan's 'giants': the Stazione Centrale, the Pirelli Building, the Stazione Garibaldi, the Cimitero Monumentale, the Fiera Campionaria and the sports facilities at S Siro. This route is best done in the morning.

– Transportation: car or Metro M1/M2 –

Today's tour is going to take in some of the busiest parts of Milan, and you'll soon realise why the city is the industrial capital of Italy.

The first stop, the **Stazione Centrale** (Central Station), is quite enormous: the facade of this huge building alone is 207m (680ft) long, and it was designed in 'Pharaonic-Neobaroque' style by the architect Stacchini in 1912 (construction work took until 1931 to complete). Although no rail journeys are planned for today, the interior is still worth a quick look. The ticket offices are completely dwarfed by their 42-m (140-ft) high facade, and in the upper part of the station the recently restored shopping area contains the **Ufficio Informazioni Turistiche** (Tourist Information Office) and also a **Duty-Free Shop** open 7.30am–9.30pm. Also spectacular is the enormous glass and metal roof spanning the platforms.

Outside once more, in the Piazza Duca d'Aosta, you are confronted by another vertical view: the **Pirelli Building**, or **Grattacielo Pirelli**. Status symbol of Milan in the 1960s and headquarters of the Pirelli administration, this 124-m (400-ft) high skyscraper today acts as an administration building for the region of Lombardy. Designed by Gio Ponti and shaped like a ship's prow, the building seems to be cutting upwards through the sky towards a more promising future.

For the rest of this route you must take the Metro, descending now to get an M2 train (*metropolitana* No 2, the so-called 'Green Line') in the direction of Romolo, and get out two stations further on at the **Stazione Garibaldi**. Here, too, a couple more Postmodernist skyscrapers will have you gazing skywards. This area is increasingly becoming a centre of administration, with the usual problem of rising rents forcing out its original inhabitants.

One place will remain unaffected by all that, though: the **Cimitero Monumentale** – and monumental it certainly is. This cemetery, situated at the end of the Via Ferrari, has a fascinating and highly morbid assortment of tombstones: Neo-Gothic, Neo-Byzantine, ultramodern and also some unbelievable, almost Hollywood-style, kitsch. Alessandro Manzoni and Carlo Cattaneo are among those to have found their final resting place here.

Leaving the cemetery, return to the Stazione Garibaldi. From there, take the M2 once again in the direction of Romolo, and then change at **Cadorna** to the M1 in the direction of Molino Dorino, getting out at the stop called **Amendola Fiera**.

Stazione Centrale

If a trade fair is taking place – and it's highly likely because the **Fiera Campionaria** is one of the most important trade fair centres in Europe – you should definitely take a look inside the exhibition buildings, where 10,000 firms vie for the attention of 5 million visitors every year.

Or otherwise you can follow the boulevard-like Via Monte Rosa with its townhouses in a southeasterly direction until you reach the **Piazza Buonarotti**, its centre adorned by a statue of Giuseppe Verdi (no one knows why the square isn't named after Verdi – except perhaps the municipal administration of Milan!). At No 9 on this Piazza is the famous building founded by Verdi in 1899 known as the **Casa di Riposo Giuseppe Verdi**, a happy home for retired musicians who, as the composer put it, were "less lucky than I". The tomb of the great man and his wife, Giuseppina Strepponi, can be seen in the funeral chapel in the grounds (ask for permission at the porter's lodge first!). Many great artists visit the Casa Verdi and the concerts held in this retirement home, which really is a happy one, have become famous.

The tomb of Giuseppe Verdi

Continue onwards on the M1 (the Metro entrance is right next to the Casa Verdi) in the direction of Molino Dorino until you reach the **Piazzale Lotto** (2 stops). You are now in the wonderful **Quartiere di S Siro** where not only the largest sporting facilities in the city, but also the magnificent villas and huge gardens belonging to the super rich Milanese are to be found.

Follow the Via Caprilli and you'll arrive right at the **Meazza Stadium**, in which Milan's two famous football teams, Inter Milan and AC Milan, play their matches (I support AC Milan, by the way). The **Parco di Trenno** behind the stadium is a good place for walks.

Back in the Metro at the Piazzale Lotto, get out two stations further on in **Lampugnano**, where you'll be met by something really rather remarkable: a mountain in Milan. Well, not quite, but the **Monte Stella**'s still a good 170m (550ft) high: it was built from the rubble left behind by World War II. Over the years it's become rather a nice park, and the Milanese even ski down its slopes in the wintertime – a snow-cannon provides the necessary slippery surface. The famous **Palatrussardi**, venue of Milan's biggest rock concerts, is also close by here. So, if you're planning to come this way again, don't forget your skis or your concert ticket!

9. Milan's Parks

Off for some fresh air! A jogging and walking tour through Milan's new parks: Forlanini, Azzurro, Zoo Preistorico.

– By car and on foot; distance: 60km (37 miles); duration: 1 day –

Today it's out into the wild green yonder away from the typical 'Milanese air'.

I should start off by mentioning that you can find several areas of green in the heart of the city, some of them created only recently, and you've actually seen some of them already: there's the **Parco Sempione**, the largest of the city's parks; the **Parco Ravizza**, not far from the elite Università Bocconì; the **Parco Lambro** on the Lambro river to the north-east, with its artificial hills; the **Parco Solari** with its ultra-modern indoor swimming pool; and last but not least, the park surrounding the **Villa Litta** to the north-west of the city. The most important areas of green, the so-called *giardini*, are of course the **Giardini Pubblici** and those at the **Villa Comunale** with its famous planetarium. There is also the **Orto Botanico** in Brera and the **Giardino Guastalla** near the *Policlinico* in the Via Francesco Sforza. The **Parco di Trenno** was laid out only quite recently in the S Siro area, and another fine place is the **Parco della Villa Reale** in Monza (a stopover on the trip to Monza, the Brianza and Lake Como).

Today involves a bit of park-hopping, but it shouldn't be too exhausting because all the destinations are situated in the same area of the map, bounded by Forlanini, the airport at Linate, the Idroscalo lake, and the Adda river. Take with you a jogging outfit and some running shoes, and for those travellers with a roof-rack, possibly a mountain-bike as well.

If you're coming from the direction of the centre and the Piazza del Duomo it's best if you start off from the Corso Porta Vittoria. First you need to drive along the Corso XXII Marzo, then take the Viale Corsica and then the Viale Forlanini, after which you go under the Tangenziale Est, and *voilà* – you've arrived at the **Parco Forlanini** on the left. The park encompasses 75,000 sq metres (18 acres) of meadow and forest, concealing several interesting and typical Lombard farms (known as *cascine*). Two of them are due to provide space for the new Botanical Garden: the **cascina Villa Landa** (Via Corelli 142) and the **cascina Case Nuove** (Via Corelli 124). Then there's the new all-purpose SAINI sports centre with its 150,000 sq metres (36 acres) providing more than enough room for almost any land-based sport you can think of.

If you prefer water, you should continue along the Via Forlanini, behind the park, to the **Idroscalo**, a 700,000 sq-metre (170-acre) artificial lake. The neighbouring park, the **Parco Azzurro**, named after the colour of the lake, is certainly worth exploring. It's the place to find a comfortable little forest clearing or a sunny meadow for a picnic. Health freaks saddle up their bicycles, speedsters head off for the Go-Kart track and swimmers stay next to the lake, where they can also take boat rides.

The lake itself is 2,500m (8,200ft) long, up to 400m (1,200ft) wide and the water is up to 4m (20ft) deep; motorboat and rowing races are held here, and in the summer the banks are crowded. If you don't fancy

In the Parco della Villa Reale

sunbathing, boating or waterskiing, you can always hire a seaplane!

Back to the car now, and it's off in the direction of Melzo along the Strade Rivoltana, which connects Segrate, Milan and San Felice. **Rivolta d'Adda** is 15km (9 miles) further on. As you can probably tell from the name, this town lies on the 313-km (195-mile) long River Adda, the banks of which are one enormous conservation area. Near its source the river flows through the Parco Nazionale dello Stelvio, and here it flows through the **Parco dell'Adda**.

The main square of Rivolta is definitely worth a visit, as is the 11th-century **Basilica di S Maria e Sigismondo** with its mighty apse and proud-looking campanile.

To the southwest of the town, on the left bank of the Adda, is the **Parco Zoo della Preistoria** (open March to November, 9am–sunset; admission). A 4-km (2.5-mile) long path here runs through forest that is jungle-like in places and, to the delight of children (and their parents), not only leads past compounds containing living animals but also lifelike scale models of dinosaurs (you'll be amazed just how large they actually were), prehistoric human settlements, cavemen, etc.

If you're feeling ready for some good food at this point, try the specialities at the **Trattoria al Capanno**: snails, venison, pork, mushrooms, and many other delicacies. The tourist menu is very reasonable, and very filling too (Tel: 0363/78024; restaurant closed on Tuesday). And this is where your excursion into the countryside comes to an end. Now it's back to the stress of the big city; I hope you'll avoid the worst of the rush hour back.

Keep fit!

10. Milan of the Future

In search of the city of the future in the area around Milan: from Segrate to Milano 2 and Milano 3 and then on to Milano Fiori, plus a detour to Cascia Vione.

– Travel by car; distance 70km (40 miles); best done in the afternoon (less traffic) –

Today's itinerary will introduce you to some of the new and ever-expanding outlying districts of Milan, with residential and business zones that are either being built or are about to be built. It's worth taking a road map, and maybe even a compass too!

The route starts in the Piazza del Duomo from where you travel in the direction of Linate, via the Corso Porta Vittoria, Piazza XXV Giornate, Corso XXII Marzo and the Viale Corsica as far as the 'Tre Ponti', or 'three-bridge' underpass which leads under the railway (the Via Piranesi, which runs parallel, contains Italy's first ever ice rink, built in 1923). Now turn into the Viale Forlanini, cross beneath the Tangenziale Est, which you'll be taking on your way back, then over the polluted Lambro river, along the side of the Parco Forlanini (see 'Milan's Parks') until you finally end up at the airport area of **Linate**.

The Viale splits into two here, and you should take the left lane signposted to **Rivoltana**, and then drive along the previously mentioned Idroscalo Lake. Straight after the Idroscalo you'll reach the municipality of **Segrate**, the loca-

Super-modern living

tion of three company buildings that can pride themselves on having what is perhaps the most expressive modern industrial architecture anywhere. The most impressive is the building belonging to the **Mondadori** publishing house: designed by architect Oscar Niemeyer and built in 1974, it is a colossal edifice made up of three sections, with the supporting part, made of reinforced concrete and with snow-white arcades, propping up the upper storeys with their offices; down in front of the building there is a friendly little lake with swans and ducks. To the right and to the left are the buildings belonging to the firm **3M** (designed by Pestalozza) and **IBM** (designed by Zanuso), both of them glass, steel and cement structures built in 1977.

Not far away from the tiny lake of Malaspina is **Milano S Felice**, the city's first purely residential suburb and also the first ever *città giardino* (garden city) in Italy (architects: Magistretti and Dominioni), with its own shopping centre and its terraced houses surrounded by parkland they are actually quite expensive to buy. Further north and not very far from the Lambro river is **Milano 2**, another spacious and elegant residential area with its own pedestrian precincts: it's a mixture of private building construction (Fininvest) and shopping centres, and over 10,000 people have made their homes here. The control centre of Silvio Berlusconi's **Canale 5**, the most well-known private TV station in Italy, is also located here.

Now travel back down the Strada Rivoltana and take the Tangenziale in the direction of Bologna. At the S Giuliano junction, where the A1 begins, you should continue along the Tangenziale (which has now become the Tangenziale Ovest i.e. west) and take the turn-off

A hungry future generation

marked Naviglio Pavese to join the Strada Statale 35. Keep to the left (SS 35 dei Giovi) in the direction of Binasco Pavia, following the 33-km (20-mile) long Naviglio Pavese that flows from Milan to Pavia; in former times it used to be an important transport route, and also provided irrigation for the fields. After a few kilometres, turn off left to Rozzano and then travel on to Basiglio.

This is the location of **Milano 3**, the most recent of the residential areas that were built during the 1980s and 90s: another 10,000 people live here, occupying a surface area of 1,700,000 sq metres (420 acres). This area is autonomous too, with its own shopping centre and several schools, and a commuter bus to the city centre which leaves every 20 minutes. Not everyone can afford to live here, however, especially at prices of around £2,000 per square metre (10.7 sq ft) of living space. Nevertheless, the whole place has a rather melancholy atmosphere to it – it's a ghetto of the wealthy with countless orange-coloured prefab terraced houses, where in the evenings (the only time of day when there's any free time) the compulsory swans in the compulsory lake are subjected to compulsory contemplation before the lights get switched off.

Close by is the **Cascina Vione**, the best-preserved 17th-century farm in the entire area, with Baroque archways, eight inner courtyards, its own chapel, a manor house and servants' quarters, stables and barns. Sixty families lived here until only very recently, supporting themselves by farming. Unfortunately the last of them will soon have to move out to make way for *nouveaux riches* and their dreams of 'doing up' country houses.

Returning to Rozzano, keep to the right in the direction of Milan. After a brief journey you will reach a fork in the road at which you should turn left in the direction of Milano Fiori-Assago. It won't be long before you arrive in the ultra-modern administrative area of **Milano Fiori**, conveniently situated between the Tangenziale Ovest and the A7 to Genoa, and probably the most futuristic modern services centre in the world. In these cleverly-designed buildings with their mirror glass facades, 12,000 people work for around 200 different firms (computer science, marketing, congress centres, etc.).

The **World Trade Centre** (architect: Renzo Piano) here is a sight worth seeing, as is the **Euromercato**, which occupies a surface area of 10,000 sq metres (107,000 sq ft). There's another enormous residential area in nearby Assago, with the gigantic **Palaforum**. But now why not take the motorway back to Milan and finish your trip into the postmodern era along the good old *navigli*, over a dish of ravioli or risotto, plus a nice glass of *Barolo* wine, in the **Ristorante Aurora** in the Via Savona? Good idea?

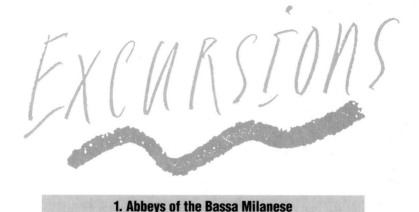

EXCURSIONS

1. Abbeys of the Bassa Milanese

A trip to three medieval abbeys to the south of Milan: Viboldone, Chiaravalle and Morimondo.

– By car; distance approximately 140km (90 miles) –

Today's excursion starts out at the Porta Romana in the direction of the Piazza Corvetto. Drive as far as the circular flower bed, where the Via Emilia, which was first laid out by the Romans, begins, and join the motorway that runs parallel, the Autostrada del Sole, a little later. On your left you'll pass the high green buildings of **Metanopoli**, one of the first satellite towns to be built after World War II.

At San Giuliano Milanese the route continues on to **Viboldone** with its abbey of the same name. It isn't a famous abbey, but is still quite enchanting architecturally; a late 12th-century red brick edifice with a unique Roman-Gothic facade, and a portal decorated with sculptures. The interior is adorned by simple 14th-century frescoes by Giusto De'Menabuoi, a great contemporary of Giotto (the *Last Judgement* above the main altar is especially striking).

Entering the Abbazia Viboldone

The abbey is the home of Benedictine nuns who run their own printing works and sell pictures of the church (visiting times 7am–12.30pm, 2.30–6.30pm). In the town itself there's very good value food to be had at the **Osteria del Ponte** (open all day every day except Saturday lunch) with its Lombard home cooking and delicious wine from the hills around Pavia.

Now go back to the nearby motorway, to S Giuliano or Sesto Ulteriano (by the way, be super-careful when studying the forest of road-signs here: you need to take the Tangenziale Ovest in the direction of Pavia). Leave at the exit marked **Vigentina** and enter the road of the same name which then turns into the

Angel in the Abbazia Viboldone

Via Ripamonti. Then take the first road off to the right (yellow sign to Chiaravalle) and a few minutes later you'll arrive in front of the famous **Abbazia di Chiaravalle** (open 9am–noon and 2–5pm), founded by Bernard de Clairvaux, and one of the largest Cistercian abbeys in Italy. The monks sell honey and delicious home-made spirits in the small shop here. The facade was redone in the 16th century: *chacun à son goût*. The interior is predominantly late 12th-century French Gothic, and the domed vault is decorated with fascinating frescoes by artists of the Giotto school. Also remarkable is the Madonna fresco by Luini (on the right hand side of the transept, at the top of a stairway) because of its *trompe l'oeil* effect, while the 14th-century campanile is particularly elegant.

Now travel back the same way you came (Tangenziale Est) and join the Autostrada dei Fiori Milano-Genova (A7), which you leave again at the second exit marked Bereguardo, following the direction of Motta Visconti/Vigevano. You're now in the **Parco del Fiume Ticino** conservation area: 90,000 hectares (220,000 acres) of officially protected fauna and flora, with groves of poplar and elm inhabited by herons, ducks and seagulls. If you feel like it you can leave the car at this point and take one of the many footpaths leading to the Ticino river, which flows right through the woods here. Should you be hungry, I strongly recommend the town of **Zelata**, situated 7km (4 miles) from the motorway: there you'll find a tiny *trattoria* with excellent home cooking, sandwiches and *Barbera* wine.

Finally you reach the grandiose **Abbazia di Morimondo**, which gets its name from its founders, Cistercian monks from Morimond in France. The abbey is a late 12th-century brick building with a simple facade and a huge rose window that bathes the interior, with its three naves and cross vault, in magnificent light on sunny days. The abbey is still inhabited by Benedictine monks, generations of whom cultivated the land around it and created the rice paddies that still exist today.

Leaving the abbey, take the left fork in the road at Ozzero to **Vigevano** (population 70,000, famous for its shoe production). Sights worth seeing here include the **Piazza Ducale**, a wonderfully harmonious square, built on the orders of Ludovico il Moro in 1494, surrounded by town houses above pillared arcades and providing a view of the impressive facade of the town's 16th-century **Duomo** (the cathedral museum contains magnificent Flemish tapestries). The **castle**, built by Bramante, is also very fine, with its 70-m (230-ft) high tower and its stables. At this point anyone who missed the last two opportunities for a good meal can eat his fill at the excellent **Al Convento** three-star garden restaurant, Via del Convento 8 (closed Tuesday).

The route back to Milan follows the road along the Naviglio Grande, through Abbiategrasso, keeping to the canal all the time until the city is reached once more at the Porta Ticinese.

Facade of the monastery of Certosa di Pavia

2. Pavia

Pavia and its hills: its Carthusian monastery, the Oltrepò Pavese and the Valtidone. A trip into the the land of the Lombards, rounded off by some very nice wines from the Oltrepò Pavese.

– By car; distance 140 kilometres (90 miles); duration 1 day –

Today you'll be taking a trip back into the depths of the Middle Ages, when the Plain of the Po was conquered by hordes of tribes from Northern Europe. The people who stayed the longest were the Lombards, and Pavia was their capital city for over 200 years: so why not find out more about them!

Setting off from the Darsena, you should follow the Naviglio Pavese as far as Binasco, and 11km (7 miles) further on you'll come to the famous Carthusian monastery, **Certosa di Pavia**. Park the car first, and then walk over to the square in front of the breathtaking facade of this building. (Opening times: 9.30–11.30am, 2.30–4.30pm; open until 5pm in March–April as well as September–October, and until 6pm in the summertime; closed Monday). The guided tours are provided by Cistercian monks, successors of the original Carthusians.

Built at the behest of Gian Galeazzo Visconti in 1396 to provide a worthy site for his family vault, the Certosa is one of the foremost monuments of the Lombard Renaissance. Priceless works of art have been collected together here over the centuries. The 15th-century facade was left incomplete, true, but that hardly diminishes its effect. The interior, half Gothic and half Renaissance, is decorated with numerous chapels and contains works by Bergognone and Perugino. Don't miss the choir in the presbytery and the ducal vault in the transept. The interior and the facade are by Amadeo. Leaving the right transept, the visitor will enter the **Small Cloister**, generously decorated with 15th-century terracotta figures, and then the **Large Cloister**, with the cells of the Carthusians ranged along its sides. Outside the refectory, directly in front of the abbey's defensive wall to the right, there is a *cascina* dating from the 18th century which today contains a wine shop (wines from the Oltrepò Pavese).

But there's not only wine – traditional *Chartreuse* is for sale here too. What *is* it, exactly? A herbal liqueur, made by monks according to the (naturally secret) original medieval recipe from Grenoble, it comes in two forms: yellow and sweet *(Chartreuse jaune)* or green and dry *(Chartreuse verte)*. The *Gra Car* on the barrels stands for '*Gratiarum Chartusia*'.

Fill the car boot with your various purchases and drive on to **Pavia**. This town on the Ticino river (population 100,000) had its heyday between the 6th and 8th century when it was the proud capital of the Lombards, and it still contains several well-preserved reminders of that time. In the 14th century the Viscontis arrived and gave this traditional university town its magnificent castle. Pavia's prosperity is due in no small measure to its agriculture as well as its clothing (especially furs) and furniture industries.

Your stroll around town will take in the following: S **Michele, Duomo, Castello dei Visconti,** and S **Pietro in Ciel d'Oro**. The best place to leave

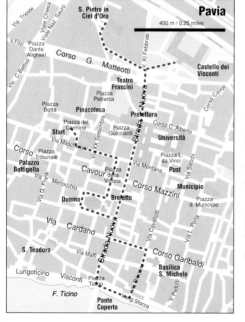

The Ponte Coperto in Pavia

the car is the Piazza del Carmine (see map), which gives access to the **Piazza della Vittoria**, lined with 14th- and 15th-century houses and arcades. One one side, behind the Duomo, is the 12th-century **Broletto** (Town Hall), and next to the Duomo, the mighty **Torre civica**, or 'municipal tower'. The **Duomo**, based on sketches by Amadeo, Leonardo and Bramante, is a fine example of the Lombard Renaissance style. Anyone who takes a look inside is sure to be impressed by the grand interior with its enormous cupola, and by the crypt (built by Bramante).

Next continue into the Strada Nuova, which at one point provides a view over the Ticino promenade and the **Ponte Coperto** bridge. The Via Diacono on the left leads to the **Basilica S Michele**, founded by the Lombards and restored in the 12th century, and probably one of the finest surviving Romanesque structures anywhere in the world. Kings and emperors were crowned here. The facade, in three sections, contains numerous human figures and fantastic creatures (note the small *loggie* above the apse and the crossing tower). The interior is remarkable for its severe beauty: three naves, with pillars and galleries. The triple-aisled crypt, supported on columns, is another highlight.

Return from S Michele to the Strada Nuova and head back to the north until the 18th-century **Teatro Frascini**, designed by Bibbiena, soon appears on your left. To the right is the 11th-century **University**, one of Europe's oldest and most respected, containing, in addition to its magnificent inner courtyards and arcades, a disused monastery. The neoclassical facade is by Piermarini and Pollock.

Three very well-preserved **Romanesque towers** can be seen on the nearby Piazza Leonardo da Vinci. And towering straight ahead is the square shape of the 14th-century **Castello dei Visconti**. The northern part was destroyed but then rebuilt after the famous Battle of Pavia in 1527. The castle contains the **Municipal Museum**, and also a **picture gallery** with works by Bellini, Boltraffio, Correggio, etc. (open 10am–noon, 2.30–5pm, but not always – it's best to ask).

From the Piazza Castello turn left along the Corso Matteotti,

Landscape near Albareto

and then once you're on the same level as the bus station, turn right towards the Romanesque church of **S Pietro in Ciel d'Oro**, consecrated in 1132. Inside this triple-naved church it's worth noting the presbytery above the crypt, and the Gothic **Arca di S Agostino** above the main altar, containing the mortal remains of St Augustine.

Return now to your car for a tour of the hilly area known as the **Oltrepò** (i.e. 'beyond the Po', as seen from the North) **Pavese**. The slopes here are crowded with vineyards and villages, and the good air means good (DOC) wine, which the vineyards bottle and sell themselves: *Bonarda, Barbera, Barbacarlo, Buttafuoco, Croatina* (red), and *Pinot, Cortese* and *Riesling* (white).

From Pavia it's also worth travelling via the towns of Casteggio, Broni and Stradella to **Castel S Giovanni** in Valtidone. The shops in the surrounding villages (Albareto, Vicomarino, Ziano Piacentino, Pianello) are stuffed full of delicacies just waiting to be discovered: *agnolotti ripieni* (a kind of ravioli with cheese filling), *tortelli* (filled with Ricotta cheese or spinach), *panzerotti* (ravioli with fresh cheese), a variety of delicious salamis and *coppa* (air-dried neck of pork).

Here are a few rewarding eating places in **Montu'Beccaria**: the **Al Pino – Da Mario Sopra Stradella** (Tel: 0385/60479, closed Tuesday afternoon and Wednesday), the **Canneto Pavese da Bazzini** (Tel: 0385/88018, closed Tuesday) or the **Stradella Ristorante Italia** (Tel: 0385/48158; overnight accommodation in comfortable, clean rooms), famed for its *brasato* (pot roast) and its *tortelli*.

3. Bergamo

A visit to one of Italy's finest towns, home of Donizetti and of the military leader Colleoni.

Bergamo Alta

– By car; distance 130km (80 miles); duration 1 day –

It's quite possible to take a bus (departing from the Piazza Castello) or a train (from the Stazione Centrale) to get to Bergamo, but as you're probably used to the car by now, why not simply take the Milan–Venice motorway and leave it almost exactly one hour later at the exit marked **Bergamo**.

This town has had quite a chequered history: at first it was a free imperial city (having joined in the fight against the Emperor Barbarossa), then it was ruled by the Viscontis, and subsequently it spent 400 years as part of the Venetian Republic – which explains the numerous lions of St Mark you'll find all over the city.

On arrival in Bergamo you can either leave your car in the *Autosilo* (multi-storey) in **Bergamo Bassa** (Piazza Giacomo Matteotti, near the Town Hall) or at the Piazza della Repubblica, in the Viale Vittorio Emanuele. From here you can walk to the *Funicolare* (funicular) terminus, situated just where the Viale Vittorio Emanuele bends, and travel up to the upper part of the city in style. Or, if you prefer, you can always park the car in front of the church of S Agostino and then stroll up along the Via Porta Dipinta, with *palazzi* to the right and left. The 13th-century Romanesque church to the left, **S Michele al Pozzo Bianco**, contains fine frescoes by the 16th-century Venetian painter Lorenzo Lotto.

As you continue uphill, the city's mighty defensive walls, built during the Venetian period, come into view: the Venetian Repub-

Santa Maria Maggiore

lic turned the city into a fortress, controlling an area that extended as far as Valtellina on the southern reaches of the Alps, with its access to the Lombardy Plain. Bastions and towers loom up on all sides, and you finally reach the **fortress** proper and the **Piazza Vecchia**, the imposing centre-piece of **Bergamo Alta** (*alta* meaning 'high', because it is nearly 400m/1,300ft above sea level). Visible from a long way off, this old part of the town is largely traffic-free and is almost unchanged since the Renaissance.

At the other end of the square is the old 12th-century **Palazzo della Ragione** with its elegant portico and Gothic triforium – sporting the lion of St Mark, naturally. The most famous buildings in the city are on this square: the **Duomo**, which has a fresco by Tiepolo in its apse, and **Santa Maria Maggiore**, a picturesque and complex 12th-century Romanesque building with magnificent portals. Opposite the presbytery is the tomb of the great opera composer Gaetano Donizetti, and also the 14th-century **Colleoni Chapel** (by the architect Amadeo), the last resting place of Bartolomeo Colleoni, the great *condottiere* (military leader) under the Venetians. Leave the church and make your way to the nearby **Piazza Mascheroni**, taking in a small detour on the way to visit the **Museo di Donizetti** in the Via Arena. Then, in the Piazza, there's the **Cittadella** with its mighty tower (formerly the residence of the Venetian governors). Passing under a large archway, you'll come to an open square called **Colle Aperto**, enclosed by the 16th-century **Porta S Alessandro**. It's here that the walk up to the **Colli di S Vigilio** (461m/1,500ft above sea-level) begins. There's

Funicular to Bergamo Alta

a ruined castle up there, and I assure you it's worth the climb for the fantastic view of gently-sloping vineyards and magnificent villas.

Walking certainly does improve the appetite, though. The specialities of this area include *polenta* (maize porridge) with songbirds, or with butter and cheese, *polenta* with sausage, *ravioli al burro* (butter ravioli), *vitello bolito* (boiled veal) and *cuore di vitello alla brace* (grilled calf's heart). The following restaurants in Bergamo Alta are definitely worth a visit: the rural **Taverna del Colleoni**, Piazza Vecchia; **La Pergola**, Borgo Canale 82, which has a terrace and a great view; or the cosy **Agnello d'Oro** (plus overnight accommodation if required), closed in January and on Monday.

After eating, you can either walk back to the Piazza S Agostino and drive down to **Bergamo Bassa** in the car, or descend in the funicular. Once you've arrived in the lower part of the town, go down the Via Pignolo until it connects with the Via S Tomaso, at the end of which you'll find the **Pinacoteca dell'Accademia Carrara** (open 9.30am–12.30pm, 2.30–5.30pm). The picture gallery is one of the most important museums in the whole of Italy: its 15 halls contain priceless works by such great masters as Pisanello, Botticelli, Mantegna, Carpaccio, Rubens, Velasquez, Dürer, Tintoretto, Tiepolo and Lotto.

Lotto was a 16th-century Venetian painter who settled in Bergamo, known for his perceptive portraits and mystical paintings of religious subjects. If you like his work, make a detour to **Trescore** and on from there to the **Villa Suardi**, 15km (9 miles) further on, where the small 14th-century church of **S Barbara**, situated in the gorgeous villa park, contains frescoes by Lotto – and the A4 motorway back to Milan is just a stone's throw away.

Eating Out

Unlike many other big Italian cities, Milan still retains its own, traditional style of cuisine, and its history can be traced right back to the Lombards. It reflects the common-sense approach of the people here: food should be good, of course, but without being unnecessarily flashy and trashy. At a recent meeting of Milanese epicures a new phrase was invented: *Slow Food*. This was a conscious reaction to dull, uninspiring fast food as well as unreliable *nouvelle cuisine*.

Slow Food means Milanese specialities: *risotto alla milanese* (with the characteristic saffron), *cotoletta* or *costoletta alla milanese, osso buco* (stuffed leg of veal), *cassoeula* (pronounced 'cassoo-urla', a very filling pork and cabbage stew) and *panettone* (cake with lemon rind and sultanas added) – to name only a few.

Of course, Milan contains restaurants to suit every palate and wallet: from self-service establishments, pizzerias and unpretentious *osterie* to the very numerous Tuscan *trattorie* with their good and relatively inexpensive food – and of course there are also the *Guide Michelin* gourmet temples.

But back to the Milanese specialities. Yellow risotto (also referred to as *risotto alla milanese* or *risotto con lo zafferano*) derives its name from its inventor, a young man called Zafferano (Saffron) in 1574. This aspiring fellow was a glazier, and liked adding a dash of saffron to his colour mixes in order to produce the shiny silvery-yellow for the windows of the Duomo (the Cathedral). This is apparently what inspired him to 'gild' the risotto he'd made his wife for their wedding day.

The recipe? I can give you the real live original recipe to serve

The Milanese yellow risotto

Trattoria Vecchia Milano

four, dating from 1821: take 8 or 9 handfuls of rice, 30 grams (1oz) of butter, 30 grams (1oz) of beef marrow or 2 teaspoons of dripping or – if you really must – 1 or 2 stock-cubes. You need 1 litre (2.1 pints) of stock, at any rate. Then a touch of saffron, 1 small onion, 20 grams (0.7oz) of dried mushrooms, and lots of (preferably fresh) Parmesan cheese. Soak the mushrooms in luke-warm water, dice the onions, fry them gently in the butter, add the marrow (or the dripping), then fry the rice with the onions briefly and give the whole thing a good stir. Now add the mushrooms and, little by little, the stock. When the rice is ready to eat you add the saffron, the ground Parmesan and butter and mix it all up to-gether. *Buon appetito!*

And now the *cotoletta alla milanese*: this is often referred to as a 'remake' of the Wiener Schnitzel, a misconception dating from the time when Milan was part of the Austro-Hungarian empire. Actu-ally it's far more likely that Governor Radetsky tasted it for the first time in Milan and was so impressed that he took it back to Vi-enna with him. The genuine *cotoletta milanese* is coated with egg and then fried in butter!

The *cassoeula*, by way of contrast, is a colourful mix of pork rib, pigs's trotter and cabbage, not for the squeamish, that's for sure. *Osso buco* and tomato go hand in hand, though – but make sure it's always knuckle of veal! Then all you need is an uncorked bottle of *Barbera*... Cheers!

Something I really should mention, by the way: prices aside, the list of restaurants that follows contains establishments that have all passed my own personal test *summa cum laude* with regard to the quality of their food, wine and service.

Key to Prices

Expensive: 100,000 lire or more per person.
Moderate to expensive: 60,000 lire or more per person.
Moderate: 40,000 lire per person.
Inexpensive: 10,000 lire per person.

Gourmet Restaurants

GUALTIERO MARCHESI
Via Bonvesin della Riva 9
Tel: 74 12 46
Closed Monday lunchtime and Sunday. Excellent fish and meat dishes with matched sauces and herbs. Expensive but definitely worth it.

LA SCALETTA
Ple Stazione di Porta Genova
Tel: 581 00 290
Closed Sunday and Monday. Run by one of the best woman cooks in Italy, Signora Pina. Moderate.

SADLER OSTERIA DI PORTA CICCA
Ripa Porta Ticinese 51
Tel: 581 04 45
Closed Sunday and Monday. Seven-course meals, very good *carpacci di tonno* (with tuna), regional cuisine. Expensive.

Milanese Cuisine

BIFFI SCALA
Piazza della Scala
Tel: 86 66 51
Closed Sunday. Futuristically designed restaurant. Chic antipasti include Iranian caviare, *risotto* and *cotoletta alla milanese*. Expensive.

LA NOS
Via Bramante 35
Tel: 331 52 63
Closed Monday and Tuesday. Milanese cuisine including *bollito* (boiled meat), *arrosto* (roasts), *filet à la Robespierre*, *torta di mele* (apple pie). Very good service. Moderate.

L'ULMET
Via Disciplini/Via Olmetto
Tel: 805 93 60
Closed Monday lunchtime and Sunday. Small restaurant with cosy atmosphere. *Tegamino di escargot* (fried snail), *tortelloni di bietola* (with beet), first-class wines. Medium to high prices.

OSTERIA CORTE REGINA
Via Rottole 60 (Via Padova)
Tel: 259 33 77
Closed Saturday lunchtime and Sunday. Owned by Nico Sivestri, journalist and gourmet. Unpretentious, delicious cuisine. Moderate.

AL PORTO
Piazzale Cantore (Darsena)
Tel: 832 14 81
Closed Sunday evening and Monday lunchtime. Fresh fish, *branzino al pepe verde* (sea perch with green pepper); white wines and the service are both first-class. Moderate.

SEIPERSEO
Via Andrea Maffei 12
Tel: 551 84 212
Closed Saturday lunchtime and Sunday. A bright restaurant with huge mirrors. Vegetarian cuisine too, plus first-class salads and *salse di tarufo* (truffle sauces). Moderate.

LE LANGHE
Corso Como 6
Tel: 655 42 79
Closed Sunday. Piedmontian restaurant offering *brasato al Barolo* (pot roast in *Barolo* wine), biscuits with warm *Zabaione*, first-class wines from the Piedmont region. Moderate.

Antipasti at the ready

Chinese

Huge selection. There's one on nearly every street corner.

Egyptian

NILO BLU
Via Padova
Tel: 284 60 67
Closed Monday. Speciality: rice with pine-cones and liver. Moderate.

French

LE MONT SAINT MICHEL
Via Poerio 3
Tel: 79 54 66
Closed Monday. Specialities from Brittany and Normandy, first-class wines. Moderate to Expensive.

Japanese

SUNTORY
Via Verdi 6
Tel: 86 22 10
Closed Sunday. Expensive.

Greek

MYCONOS
Via Tofane 5
Tel: 261 02 09

TRATTORIA MILANESE
Via Santa Marta 11
Tel: 86 45 19 91
Closed Tuesday. A classic Milanese *trattoria* with nostalgic atmosphere, antipasti and turn-of-the-century interior. *Nervetti* (boiled calf's head with mixed pickles), *pesciolini in carpione* (fish in a doughnut with raisins and wine), *minestrone alla milanese* (vegetable soup), *risotto al salto* (with paprika and peas), *osso buco, panettone* and Lombard wines. Moderate.

American

JULEP'S NEW YORK
Via Torricelli 21
Tel: 894 90 29
Closed Wednesday, only open evenings. Good meat dishes. Moderate.

Brazilian

BERIMBAU
Via de Andreis 13
Tel: 701 02 800
Food provided is excellent. Music after 10pm. Moderate.

Closed Tuesday, only open in the evenings. Very Greek. Inexpensive.

Lebanese

ACCADEMIA
Via Accademia 53
Tel: 289 15 69
Closed Sunday. Kitchen closes at 11pm. Good meat. Inexpensive.

Russian

YAR
Via Mercalli 22
Tel: 54 80 53
Closed Sunday. Original Russian cooking. Moderate to Expensive.

Spanish

TABERNA VASCA
Via Lodovico il Moro 63
Tel: 81 94 02
Closed Monday. Typical Spanish cuisine. Moderate.

Thai

PATTAYA
Via Muratori 10
Tel: 55 18 93 26
Closed Monday. Skewered meat with coconut. Inexpensive.

Hungarian

UNGHERESE
Largo la Foppa 5
Tel: 659 94 87
Closed Sunday. Hearty Hungarian home cooking. Moderate.

Vegetarian

JOIA
Via Castaldi 18
Tel: 204 92 44
Closed Saturday lunchtime and Sunday. First-class vegetarian food served in two rooms (smoking/non-smoking), fixed menu. Moderate.

Pizzerie

The *pagine gialle* (yellow pages) will give you the addresses of the CALAFURIA chain (Tel: 86 61 03), who know how to bake a good crusty pizza. Another good place is

LA CUCCUMA
Via Pacini 26
Tel: 266 49 45
Closed Sunday lunchtime and Tuesday. Excellent pizza and *pizza calzone*. Inexpensive.

Restaurants for Young People

Milan's *paninari* (young people) have been satisfying their hunger at the city's so-called *paninoteche* since the beginning of the 1980s with sandwiches and rolls, and quenching their thirst with beer or coke – at student prices, naturally (around 10,000 lire). I recommend the *paninari* among you to visit the area around the *navigli*, where there's a lot going on in the evening.

Or perhaps you'd prefer fast food?

Around the cathedral square you'll find **BURGHY** (Milan kids love it!) with hamburgers, chips and fizzy drinks. You can find outlets at Piazza Duomo 17, Piazza Cordusio, or Via Vittorio Emanuele 26. There's fast food from **WENDY'S**, too, which has actually broadened its selection to include pasta dishes, (fruit) salads and yoghurts; Piazza Argentina (closed Tuesdays) or Piazza Duca d'Aosta (closed Mondays). **ITALY ITALY** is the Italian answer to the challenge from America, and offers pasta dishes with Southern Italian sauces (Via Stampa 14, Via Torino/Carobbio).

Self-service at 10,000 Lire

There are so-called *tavole calde* all over the place for people in a hurry at lunchtime: the chain called **AMICO DELLA MOTTA**, for instance, where you can just have an icecream or drink a cup of tea if you like (Via Piazza Duomo 1/Via Orefici).

Midnight Dining

The nightlife capital of Italy always has food prepared for nocturnal prowlers, in restaurants, cabarets, live music bars or piano bars. There's no official closing time here, you see: those who stay on, stay on.

AL GARIBALDI
Via Monte Grappa 7
Tel: 659 80 06
Open till 4am, closed Friday. Rendezvous point for people from showbiz, politics and the fashion world. Pleasant atmosphere. Moderate to Expensive.

BE BOP
Via Col di Lana 4
Tel: 837 69 72
Open till 4am, closed Sunday. Young, friendly atmosphere. Fantastically good salads. Moderate.

ALFREDO
Via Borghese 14
Tel: 331 90 00
Closed Sunday; closes between 3 and 4am (depending on clientele). Run by Alfredo Valli, one of the greats of Milan gastronomy. A very elegant establishment. Moderate to Expensive.

HAPPY ROCK
Via Casale 7 (navigli area)
Tel: 581 12 220
Open 10pm–2.30am, closed Tuesdays. Lots of eating, drinking and chatting. Moderate.

Something to suit every taste

Snack bars, piano bars, pubs, cafés...

AL TEATRO/BAR
Corso Garibaldi 16
Tel: 86 42 22
Open 7pm–2am, closed Monday. The right place to meet up after a theatre evening, Bohemian atmosphere, black music in the evenings. Moderate.

BAR MARGHERITA
Via Moscova 25
Tel: 659 08 33
Closed Sunday; open midnight–2 am. In the Brera/Garibaldi area. Pleas-

ant atmosphere, not at all hectic. First-class selection of spirits (40 different types of whisky and grappa). Hot and cold dishes. Live jazz in the evenings. Moderate to Expensive.

DINNER & LUNCH CLUB
Via Solferino 48
Tel: 657 16 08
Open 1–3pm, 7.30pm–1am. A tiny breakfast and lunch bar with a delicatessen attached. Twin establishment in London. Moderate.

PORTNOY CAFFÉ LETTERARIO
Via de Amicis 1/Corner of Corso Porta Ticinese
Tel: 837 86 56
Open 7pm–2am, closed Sunday. A meeting place for poets and writers who hold their debates in the small salon (first floor). Art exhibitions. Musicians introduce their own songs. Cocktails and long drinks with cold snacks and sandwiches. Moderate.

Piano Bars

Eat your food to the sound of virtuoso solo pianists or small combos:

CALIMERIUS
Via San Calimero 3
Tel: 58 30 97 02
Open 6pm–3am, closed Sunday. Quiet, elegant atmosphere. Live music plus first-class snacks and cocktails. Just the place for young lovers. Medium priced.

MOMUS
Via Fiori Chiari 8
Tel: 805 62 27
Open 8pm–2am, closed Sunday. Situated in the heart of the Brera. Very elegant. A singer and a pianist entertain daily until closing time. Prior reservation essential! Moderate.

Cabaret

Milan has a long cabaret tradition extending back as far as the *Risorgimento* period (mid-19th century). Several famous stars began their careers here in Milan, too, including Dario Fo, Gaber, Franca Valeri and Paolo Rossi. Most of the city's cabarets are in the *navigli* area.

CAPOLINEA
Via Lodovico il Moro 119
Tel: 89 12 20 24
Closed Monday. Satire, music. Moderate.

CA' BIANCA
Via Lodovico il Moro 117
Tel: 813 52 60
Closed Sundays. Private club. Annual membership costs 50,000 lire. International cabaret. Moderate.

DERBINO MILANO
Via Missaglia 46
Tel: 846 47 31
Open Thursday, Friday and Saturday.

Discos and Dancing

Places to grind and sweat.

GOOD MOOD
Via Turati 29
Tel: 29 00 33
Open 9pm–2.30am, closed Monday. Suitable dress required. Music sometimes live.

LA PORTA D'ORO
Piazza Diaz 3
Open until 4am. Revues direct from Paris, capital of all things naughty.

Live Music and Shows

AMNESIE
Via Cellini 2
Tel: 540 09 58
Open 11pm–3am, closed Monday. Meeting point for models and the fashionable set. American music.

PALASHOW
Via di Vittorio Metropol 2
Tel: 92 10 15
Open 10pm–3am, closed Sunday, Tuesday, Wednesday. Very large establishment, offering almost everything from standard dance all the way to rock music.

TIME
Via Massarani 6
Tel: 639 73 47
Thursday–Sunday 10.30pm–2am. Megadisco, rendezvous point for young from the country, heavy metal addicts and skinheads. Cheap.

AMERICAN DISASTER
Via Boscovich 48
Open Thursday, Friday, Saturday 10pm–3am. A cross between a disco and a piano bar. John Travolta-like atmosphere. Drag shows on Sundays.

Milano Erotica

EL MAROCCO
Via Baracchini 1
Open until 4am, closed Sunday. Striptease, ballet and games.

SCIMMIE
Via Ascanio Sforza 49
Tel: 89 40 28 74
Open 8 pm–2 am, closed Tuesday. Half *birreria* (pub) and half restaurant. On the Naviglio Pavese with tables on a barge. First-class music programme, with groups and artists alternating nightly.

TANGRAM
Via Pezzotti 52
Tel: 89 50 10 07
Open 9pm–2am, closed Sunday. Everything from funk to jazz, and from rock to fusion.

ZELIG
Viale Monza
Tel: 255 17 74
Open 9 pm–2 am, closed Monday. Mixture of live music and cabaret. The bar is good.

CAFÉ TEATRO NOBEL
Via Ascanio Sforza 81
Open 9pm–2am, closed Tuesday. Attractive cocktail of shows, jazz, theatre and cabaret. Dancing to live music.

Check through the 'what's on' listings in the major dailies such as *La Repubblica* or *Corriere delle Sera*; or you can also consult the special list of events published by the city itself, available from kiosks.

Cinema

Most first performances tend to be screened in the cinemas along the Corso Vittorio Emanuele and the surrounding area (**Abasciatori, Gloria, Excelsior**, and also the huge **Odeon** cinema which has now been subdivided into eight smaller ones). The best place for original-language films is the **Angelicum**; first-run films can be seen at **Centrale 1** and **2** (Via Torino 30) or in **De Amicis** (Via de Amicis 34). For art movies, try the **Cineteca Museo** (Cinema Palazzo Dugnani, Via Manin 2a).

Music

Besides La Scala, the most famous opera house in the world, there are a few other centres of music: there's the city-owned **Angelicum** (Piazza S Angelo) with its own symphony orchestra; the **Chiesa di S Marco** (Piazza S Marco 2), where Mozart once lived – religious music; the **Civica Scuola di Musica** (Via Stilicone 36), where the emphasis is on contemporary music in particular; the **Conservatorio di Musica Giuseppe Verdi** (Via Conservatorio 12), a former monastery, stages afternoon concerts; and last but not least there's the **Musica e Poesia a S Maurizio** (Church of S Maurizio on the Corso Magenta) for ancient and Baroque music.

Theatre

Theatres financed with either public or private money in Milan include the **Piccolo Teatro** (Via Rovello 2), founded by Giorgio Strehler and Paolo Grassi, and my own 'personal' theatre for many years now; it also has another offshoot, the **Teatro Studio** (Via Fossati), and construction of a second one with 1,200 seats is planned next door to it. The **Dell'Elfo** (Via Ciro Menotti 11) used to be a cinema, and is run by one of Italy's most interesting theatre cooperatives; the **Delle Marionette** (Via degli Olivetani 3b) features Italy's most successful puppet theatre troupe (the Colla brothers, who have been in the business for two centuries); and the **Manzoni** (Via Manzoni 42) is a traditional theatre dating from 1850 with one of the finest foyers around.

Off off-theatre stands for theatre, music, cabaret, dance and cinema: **Anteo** (Via Milazzo 9); **Ciak** (Via Sangallo 33); **Teatrotenda MM** (in Lampugnano), the Milan rock temple, also known as 'Palatrussardi''; CRT (Via Dini 7, tram No 15), outside the centre, famous for its avant-garde theatre troupes; OUT OFF (Via Dupré 4, bus lines 90 and 91), avant-garde; and the rather unusual **Buratto** (Corso Garibaldi) which does its own children's productions.

A wide variety of events take place in Milan almost every day of the year. Notable is the **Fiera di Sinigaglia** which takes place on the banks of the Darsena sui Navigli every Saturday, and the **Mercatone dell'Antiquariato** (last Sunday of every month except for July and August), also on the banks of the Navigli. For information about events in the Trade Fair Centre ring the APT on 87 00 16 or 80 96 62. For information on art exhibitions, contact the Ufficio Stampa Assessorato alla Cultura del Comune di Milano, Via Marino 7, Tel: 623 61.

JANUARY

6 January: *Corteo dei Re Magi* (Epiphany). Procession of the Three Kings from the Piazza del Duomo to the Church of S Eustorgio.

Mid-January: *Esposizione internationale canina di Milano* (Trade Fair Centre). More information on the International Dog Show can be obtained from Gruppo Cinofilo Milanese, Viale Premuda 21, Tel: 76 00 88 14, Fax: 76 01 49 35.

Triennale di Milano. Start of a series of events based on the theme of 'living with things and with nature' which continues until mid-April.

FEBRUARY

All month: *Carnevale Ambrosiano* and *sfilate di moda*, fashion fairs held in the Trade Fair Centre.

End of February: *Borsa internazionale del turismo* (Trade Fair Centre). More information: Expo CTS, Via Serbelloni 2, Tel: 76 00 73 25, Fax: 78 18 28.

MARCH

March/April: *Organ concerts* in S Maurizio and S Simpliciano. A similar series takes place in the autumn.

End of March: *Milanofil* (Trade Fair Centre). Major philately exhibition.

APRIL

Mid-April: *Mostra di pittura 'l'arte al*

cielo aperto'. This unusual open-air art fair has been held in the Via Bagutta since 1963. During its two days in spring and autumn it attracts over 200,000 people.

Salone internazionale del mobile (Trade Fair Centre). More information on the Milan Car Fair can be obtained from: Cosmit, Corso Magenta 96, Tel: 48 00 87 16, Fax: 481 35 80.

APRIL/MAY

Sussurri e grida. Literally, 'whispering and shouting' – productions by the city's avant-garde theatres.

Festival internazionale del Jazz 'Città di Milano'. The high point of the Milan jazz scene.

Internazionale dell'antiquariato (Trade Fair Centre). More information on the antiques fair is available from: EXPO CTS, Via Serbelloni 2, Tel: 771 81, Fax: 78 18 28.

MAY

Danza a teatro. Dance performances take place in various theatres throughout the month.

Estate all'idroscalo. Start of the summer festival at the *Idroscalo* with sport, folklore and exhibitions.

Milano Aperta. From May to June and October to November, Milan hosts several high-quality international theatre performances.

First week in May: *Festa del Santo Chiodo*. Masses are held at the Duomo as part of the 'Festival of the Holy Nail.'

Last Sunday in May: *Sagra del Carroccio*. A procession in historic costume. The *palio*, a kind of religiously motivated race, is held in Legnano.

JUNE

First Sunday in June: *Festa dei Navigli*. Folklore, music and entertainment by the *navigli* and the Darsena.

Third Sunday in June: *Festa di S Luigi*; *Salone Internazionale del Golf* (Trade Fair Centre). More information from: PGM Italia SRL, Via Fontanili 3, Tel: 89 50 29 20.

JUNE/JULY

Milano estate. The 'Summer in Milan' festival: cultural events, music, theatre and dance.

Musica nei Cortili. Classical concerts in a selection of Milan's finest courtyards.

Milanese sweet declarations of love

AUGUST

Vacanze a Milano. 'Holidays in Milan' festival.

SEPTEMBER

La Moda a Milano. Fashion shows and events.
First week in September: *Festa del Santo Chiodo.* The 'Holy Nail' festival is

Fish for Christmas

held for a second time.
From September onwards there are ballet and concert performances in La Scala (the opera season proper only starts on 7 December).

OCTOBER

Mostra di pittura 'l'arte al cielo aperto'. The year's second two-day-long open-air art market in the Via Bagutta.
Milano oltre. Festival of theatre, dance, music and 'more' (*'oltre'*).
Milano poesia. International poetry festival.
Limitrofie. Latest developments in art, theatre and jazz.
> **First Sunday in October:** *Festa di Chiaravalle.*
> **Last Sunday in October:** *Sagra del Tartufo.* This *'sagra* of the truffle' takes place in the Via Ripamonti.

NOVEMBER

> *Mercato degli antiquari Milanesi.* Annual meeting of the city's guilds, in the Palazzo della Permanente.
> *Premio letterario Bagutta.* One of the most important prizegiving ceremonies in the Italian literary world.

DECEMBER

> **7 December:** *Festa di S Ambrogio.* Festival of the city's patron saint, with processions, masses and markets.
> *Fiera degli Oh bei, Oh bei.* This superior flea market begins on the same day, in the Piazza S Ambrogio.

7 December: Season opens at La Scala.
Third week in December: *Natale in Darsena.* A Christmas market, featuring special events and old Christmas customs, is held on the Darsena until 6 January.

Shopping

To start off with, let's define our terms: 'shopping' in Milan means the same as it does in any other capital city in Europe, i.e. enjoying a pleasant, relaxed stroll, and giving one's eyes a treat above all, while possibly fulfilling some long-cherished desire in the process. Key shopping areas are the **Piazza del Duomo** and its environs: **Corso Vittorio Emanuele**, **Via Torino**, **Via Montenapoleone**, **Via della Spiga**, **Via S Andrea**, **Via Santo Spirito**, **Via Borgospesso**, **Corso Buenos Aires**, **Via Paolo Sarpi**, **Corso Vercelli** and **Corso XXII Marzo**. You'll find absolutely everything in this section of the map, from the *Rinascente* Megastore to boutiques, sportswear shops, gourmet food outlets, antique shops, gift shops, jewellers, carpet stores... *basta!*

Bookshops *(librerie)*

Since Milan is the capital of Italian publishing, and each publishing house runs its own separate bookstore, you have a huge selection: **Bocca,** Corso Vittorio Emanuele 2, has excellent art books and is a real treasure trove for book lovers; **Einaudi**, Via Manzoni 40, is a very popular Milanese bookshop; **Feltrinelli**, Via Manzoni 12, has a very good selection, including a lot of foreign-language literature and international newspapers; **Hoepli**, Via Hoepli 5, is the largest bookstore in Italy, covering 4 floors, with a good assortment of specialist books on management, computing and science; **San Babila**, Corso Monforte 2, is the best address for art books, and the staff are very competent; **Il Polifilo**, Via Borgonuovo 3, an antique bookshop for rare finds taken from former 18th-century libraries; **Libreria del Corso**, Corso Buenos Aires 49, Milan's leading fiction bookshop, very large, with its own conference terrace; **Rizzoli**, Galleria Vittorio Emanuele

Culinary specialities

79, sublime atmosphere, travel guides, teaching materials, conference hall.

The city doesn't have all that many foreign-language bookshops. There's **The American Bookstore**, Largo Cairoli/Via Camperio, where you can find anything in English or American; or **The International Bookshop**, Via Senato 28, the Oxford School's official bookshop, which also has a lot of books in Spanish; and there's also the **Librairie Française**, Via S Pietro all'Orto 10.

Hairdressers

Aldo Coppola, Via Manzoni 25, is a real pleasure, with 30 young lads in white aprons washing, cutting, combing and colouring; **Pierre**, Via Rovello 8, is a great place to relax while a veritable swarm of young girl hairdressers set upon your shaggy locks – Loredana Bertè and Eros Ramazotti are clients here; **Annette e Mario**, Via S Andrea 2 (the very best hairstyles at the Scala-Gala are always compositions by Annette); **Benito**, Via Rovello 1, just does men (and, ahem, includes such VIP customers as myself, and the prices are very reasonable, too. Hairdressers are always closed on Monday.

Contact Lenses/Glasses

Studio Lenti a Contatto, Piazza Missori 3, gives good advice and does fittings. **Aspesi**, Largo Richini 1, has been in the optical business since 1910. Or there's also **Galileo**, Corso Garibaldi 113.

Delicatessens

You've already had a chance to experience **Peck**, the ultimate in Milanese gastronomy, during your stroll down the Via Torino (page 34); fortunately for the taste buds, though, Peck is by no means the only place in town! **Il Salumaio**, Via Montenapoleone 12, the only establishment in this street that isn't a fashion shop, is filled with gastronomic delights and also has a French and Italian *enoteca* (wine selection); **Parini**, Via Borgospesso 1, estd. 1918, is the place to go for biscuits and sugar-free cakes, and it also has 200 different kinds of beer; **Sant'Ambroeus**, Corso Matteotti 7, is the *non plus ultra* (why not buy an original souvenir here – an ice-cream sculpture for instance?); **Arte Bianca**, Corso Monforte 18, has everything that can be produced using flour, including a huge selection of breads, biscuits and cakes, fresh noodles, ravioli and *focacce* (thin flaky pastries with or without filling); **Formaggia**, Via Larga/corner of Santa Tecla, is

Mortadella from the hook

legendary among Milan's *drogherie*, with its first-class perfume assortment and its fine wines; **Poporoja**, Via Eustachi 17, does oriental specialities including fish pasta and jellyfish in brine, as well as a tray of Japanese delicacies *(sushi, bento)*; and **Leoni**, Corso Venezia 7/1, is a Milanese institution (also open Sunday) where you can get just about everything, including delicious stuffed vegetables.

The grace of every living room

Been invited anywhere? Don't forget to bring a present!

Milan has a lot of shops containing gifts for those 'who have everything'. **Arform**, Via della Moscova 22, has a huge assortment of gifts and arts and crafts; **La Tenda**, Via Solferino (under the arcades), does everything for women; **Coruna**, Via Santo Spirito 19, has some superb patience-trying games to give to fussy friends; **Controbuffet**, Via Solferino 14 and **Penelope**, Via Solferino 12, both contain the ultimate in gifts. And in case you're still wondering what on earth to get after all this you can always head for **Gucci**, Via Montenapoleone 5, where you're certain to find what you want in the huge basement.

Hats, Luggage, Shoes…

Melegari, Via P. Sarpi 19, does hats for men and women including such brand names as Borsalino, Stetson and Christy's; **Rossi Daniele**, Galleria Vittorio Emanuele 16, does Barbisio, Bantam and Stetson; **Valigeria Brovelli**, Via Vitruvio 38, does Samsonite aluminium suitcases and fine luggage; **Figus Design**, Via Cerva 14, one of the best leather shops in town, produces its own wares and does a good line in belts; **Il Passatempo**, Via Montevideo 9, is a beautifully laid-out shop and is very exclusive; **Abbigliamento Osé**, Via Spallanzani 6 (near the Corso Buenos Aires), does tight-fitting stuff, thin veils, etc.; **Borsalino**, Corso Vittorio Emanuele 5, is *the* international place to go for hats; **Di Varese**, Corso Vittorio Emanuele 9, is one of the oldest and most respected shoeshops.

Records, Tapes & CDs

Milan is the capital of the Italian music publishing world, and the publishing house of **Casa Ricordi** looks after some of the best international musicians (and also owns the rights to Verdi's entire opus). **Ricordi**, Via Berchet 2, has shelves of LPs, tapes, CDs, scores, piano reductions and musical instruments both electronic and traditional, all at acceptable prices; **Messaggerie Musicali**, Corso Vittorio Emanuele 2, does musical instruments, scores and books on music; **Buscemi**, Corso Magenta 31, is a favourite haunt of Anglo-American hi-fi music fans; **The Black Saint**, Via Monti 41, is an almost inexhaustible treasure trove for jazz fans; **Metropolis**, Via Padova 14, is a rock music centre; and **Il Discomane**, Alzaia Naviglio Grande 36, is a second-hand shop with some very rare records.

Dry Cleaners
Unfortunately there isn't a single 24-hour dry cleaners anywhere in proud Milan. Anyone who doesn't mind parting with his or her favourite item over the lunch-break, though, should visit any of the following *lavanderie a secco* (dry cleaners): **Mack Rapid**, Viale Premuda 34 (open 8.30am–12.30pm and 2.30–7.30pm); **Lavarapido**, Via Tolstoi 15 (open 8.30am–12.30pm and 3.30–7.30pm, express service only on Mondays). Coin-operated laundries *(Lavanderie a gettoni selfservice)* include **Automatica**, Via Neera 14 (open 8.00am–12.30pm and 2.30–7.00pm); and **Osmetti**, Viale Monte Nero 50 (open 8.30am–12.30pm and 3.30–7.30pm, also Saturday mornings).

Second Hand
Looking for that unbelievable bargain? A tailcoat, cloak or dinner jacket? Then drop in at **Baule**, Via Vetere 12, or try **Surplus**, Corso Porta Ticinese 101. You want even *more* of a selection?! Well, in that case the place to go is definitely the **USA Shop**, Via San Maurilio 2, with its 20s clothing, Marlene Dietrich-style hats, punk and new-wave outfits, etc.

Sports Goods
Ever since Ronald Reagan donned a jogging outfit and the Pope was photographed skiing, sports shops have been springing up all over Milan. Another reason is certainly the large selection of fitness centres, swim-

Milan's second-hand bookshops are always worth a look

ming pools, tennis courts, etc as well as a Milanese habit: the weekend is sacred! (They go skiing in the Aosta valley, surfing on the Adriatic, sailing on the lakes, rowing on the *droscelo*...). **Brigatti**, Corso Vittorio Emanuele 67, with its huge selection of sports goods from golf clubs to baseball masks, is the place to go for Milan's 'in' set (though the prices aren't all that sporting); **Germani Sport**, Corso Vittorio Emanuele 2, has a big selection and very good swimsuit fashions; **Peter Sport**, Piazzetta Liberty 8, right next to the Duomo, does interesting diving gear and also racquets, bags etc. in all sizes and colours at reasonable prices; **Italo Sport**, Corso Vercelli 11, does absolutely everything, though it's expensive; **Sport Fortuna**, Foro Buonaparte 57, does fitness accessories, and skiing, tennis, swimming, hunting and fishing equipment at reasonable prices; and **Zinetti Sport**, Piazza Bacone 7, does everything too, and is also good value.

'*Drogherie*'

These are a Milanese speciality and have absolutely nothing to do with drugs. *Drogherie* are the Italian version of grocer's shops where you can find absolutely everything, from soap to fine whisky and from diet food to mothballs. Here's a list of the most reasonably-priced ones: **Ferrari**, Via Ponte Vetero 14, has rare balsamic vinegar *(aceto balsamico)*, wines, soap from Marseilles, jams, etc.; **La Coloniale**, Corso Genova 19, has jams, preserves, spirits, washing powder, etc.; **Parini**, Via Borgospesso 1, same as above plus a great assortment of sugar-free cake and also 200 different kinds of beer (including German *Schaff* beer, fermented in oak casks and sold in numbered bottles) as well as *extravergine* olive oil; **British Grocery**, Viale Beatrice d'Este 48, run by Danny Gattoni, is great for tea and also sells real English beer-glasses!

Milan's Markets

I will spare you details of the so-called *ipermercati* (there's one in Milano Fiori that's as large as the Piazza del Duomo). Then there are the *supermercati* (Esselunga, 25 branches; A&O, 50 branches; and there's a Standa or an Upim on nearly every street corner). I can't give you a list of opening times because each chain is different. As far as department stores are concerned, the most famous one is probably **La Rinascente**, next to the Duomo, with its extremely French display windows (designed by Bernard). Very typical of Milan, though, are the traditional markets – known as *mercatini all'aperto* and *mercatini comunali* – and the city has around 11,000 of them altogether. You can find out when and where they are taking place by checking the newspapers. Traditional markets include the **Fiera di Sinigallia** at the Darsena dei Navigli, where various objects and antiques are offered for sale every Sunday until 1pm, and the **Mercatone dell'Antiquariato**, a kind of Milanese folk festival, which is held along the Naviglio Pavese and the Naviglio Grande on the last Saturday in each month.

The *mercatini comunali* take place in various quarters of the city and there you can find food, household equipment, fish, etc. These markets are very popular with the Milanese, not least because of the very reasonable prices charged (market hours are 8.30am–1pm and 4–7.30pm). I would personally recommend the *mercatino* in the Piazza XXIV Maggio, because of the phenomenal selection.

PRACTICAL Information

When to Visit

The climate in Milan, like that of the Lombardy Plain as a whole, is damp the whole year through – hot and sticky in summer, hazy and foggy in winter. The horizon is generally grey, and good visibility is rare. Don't let that discourage you, however, because after all, it's the people who make the place. If you're lucky with the weather, though, you'll experience superb days in spring and in late autumn. That's when the Alps seem to be right under your nose from the roof of the Duomo, with visibility extending perhaps even as far as Monte Rosa.

I'd recommend you to visit Milan at the end of April or the beginning of May, when windy days ensure that there's good visibility, or in August, when the city is empty because everyone is on holiday (though a lot of restaurants and shops are closed at this time too). September, when the city gradually gets back into its stride, has its own special charm too.

Arrival by Car

'Gridlock' is another Milanese spe-ciality. Rule number one for anyone who wants to save himself endless stress and trouble is leave your car in the hotel car park. The city can quite easily be explored via the public transport system. You only really need a car to explore the outlying areas, or to reach the suburbs quickly.

The **Azienda Trasporti Municipalli** (ATM), the municipal transport system, has a series of supervised car parks along the major arterial roads leading into the city. Electronic signboards give information on the nearest car parks and how many spaces are left. Thus, anyone arriving via the motorways or major roads can park his or her car safely at the various public transport termini (eg of the *metropolitana* Metro system).

There are many ways of reaching Milan, and it's worth summarizing them briefly:

Anyone approaching Milan from the south (from Bologna/Rome) arrives in the city along the *Autostrada del Sole*, while the *Autostrada Torino/Venezia* brings in travellers from the west (Turin) and the east (Venice). From Genoa, to the south-west, there is the *Autostrada di Genova*, and from the lakes to the north there is the *Autostrada del Laghi* (Como/Varese). **A1:** *Autostrada del Sole* (information

Tel: 35 44 051); from and to Bologna and the Adriatic coast.

A4: *Autostrada Serenissima* (information Tel: 35 44 051); from and to Bergamo, Brescia, Verona (connecting on to the Brenner Pass), Vicenza, Padua, Venice (connecting on to Vittorio Veneto, Pordenone, Udine and Trieste).

A4: From and to Turin (information Tel: 35 31 223), connecting with the Aosta valley.

A7: From and to Genoa and the Italian Riviera (information Tel: 84 35 910). In the city it's a normal street, then it separates into three motorway sections as far as the Swiss border.

Superstrada No 36: Lecco, Sondrio, Valltellina. Connection on to Monza if you're coming from the A4.

Tangenziale Est: This feeder road to the east connects Metanopoli and Linate (the airport) with the south of the city (connecting on to the Autostrada del Sole).

Tangenziale Ovest: Feeder road to the west, connecting the south (connection to *Autostrada del Sole*) with the northbound A8, via the Porta Ticinese and San Siro.

Tangenziale A4 Turin/Venice: The motorway acts as a feeder and provides a connection with Monza via the Viale Zara. In Agrate it joins the Tangenziale Est and continues on towards Venice.

A word of warning, though: permanent road works, hopeless overcrowding and bad signposting (even Rome's *raccordo annulare* pales in comparison) have turned the *tangenziali* into a veritable nightmare for those unfamiliar with them.

Assuming you've found your way into Milan, you now need to find somewhere to park. The information office of the ATM can help you further (Tel: 890 107 97 or 669 7032, 8.00am–8pm except public holidays) should

you experience any difficulties with the following car parks:

Car parks to the north-east: Take the exit on the *Autostrada Venezia* near the *Tangenziale Est* (A4)

Cascina Gobba: 1,800 spaces, also open at night (connection: Metro line 2)

Cologno Nord: 900 spaces (connection: Metro line 2)

Crescenzago: 600 spaces (connection: Metro line 2)

Forlanini: 600 spaces (connection: Bus 73 to Linate airport and the Metro system)

Gesate: 500 spaces (connection: Metro line 2)

Car parks to the north: Near the *autostrada* A4 to Venice and the Autostrada dei Laghi junction (A8, A9).

Sesto Marelli: 250 spaces (connection: Metro line 1)

Lampugnano: 2,200 spaces, also open at night (connection: Metro line 1)

Molino Dorino: 250 spaces (connection: Metro line 1)

Car parks to the south: On the *Tangenziale Ovest* and at the exit from the *autostrada* from Genoa (A7).

Romolo: 250 spaces (connection: Metro line 2)

Bisceglie: 1,900 spaces; closed 10pm–7am (connection: Metro line 1)

Private car parks in the city centre: Autosilo Repubblica: *Piazza Repub-*

blica 14, Tel: 659 79 96 (24 hours).
Autosilo Diaz: *Piazza Diaz 6 (very close to the Duomo), Tel: 864 60 077,* open 7.30–1am.
Autosilo Gorizia: *Via Gorizia 14 (on the Darsena dei Navigli), Tel: 581 063 98,* open 6.30–1.30am.

Autosilo Nerino:
Via Nerino 6, Tel: 805 67 25 (24 hours).
Petrol stations open at night:
AGIP: *Piazzale Accursio,* 10pm–7am; *Viale Marche 32,* 10pm–1am.
Esso: *Viale Liguria 12,* 10pm–7am; *Piazzale Baracca,* 10pm–1am.

By Train

Anyone arriving by train in Milan will arrive at the Central Station (Stazione Centrale), the Stazione Piazza Duca d'Aosta, the Stazione Garibaldi or the Stazione Lambrate. Metro lines 1 and 3 will then take you into the centre and to the Piazza del Duomo.

The central station was given a facelift for the World Cup in 1990. The platforms are up on the first floor, where you can also find Travel Information (Tel: 67 500), a bank (Banca delle Communicazioni, open 8am–7pm Monday–Saturday) and a 24-hour pharmacy. There's also a Selfservice here if you're feeling hungry (11.30am–10pm), and a Duty Free Shop (7am–9.30pm).

The Italturismo tourist office (open 7am–8pm) is on the ground floor by the entrance to the Metro. The Albergo Diurno ('day hotel') can provide you with a quiet room, luggage service, a bar, hairdresser, manicure and pedicure service, drugstore, dry cleaning service (it takes a day though), hot mangle, photocopier, bath, showers and toilets. Next to the tourist office (where, by the way, you can get train tickets without having to queue) is the post office.

By Plane

Milan has two airports: the international one, **Forlanini Linate**, and the intercontinental one, **Malpensa**. In emergencies, or if it's foggy, there's a third one too: **Orio in Serio**, near Bergamo.

Linate was substantially improved for the World Cup in 1990:
General Information: Tel: 748 52 200
Domestic Arrivals: Tel: 738 21 31
International Arrivals: Tel: 738 723
Domestic and International Departures: Tel: 738 05 01
Lost and Found: Tel: 738 44 51
Car Hire:
AVIS: Tel: 717 214
EUROPCAR: Tel: 738 272
HERTZ: Tel: 738 45 80
Getting to Linate airport: There's a shuttle bus service run by the Municipal Rail Service (Ferrovie dello Stato FS) every 20 minutes from the central station, from 5.40am until the last flight. The ATM bus 73 travels regularly from the front of the airport (Piazzale del Aeroporto) to its terminus on the Piazza S Babila/corner of Corso Europa.

The airport at **Malpensa**, a full 40km (25 miles) away from the city centre, is still waiting for a train connection:
General Information: Tel: 748 52 200
Lost and Found: Tel: 748 54 215
Car Hire:
AVIS: Tel: 868 019
EUROPCAR: Tel: 868 017
HERTZ: Tel: 868 001
Getting to Malpensa airport: The FS shuttle bus departs very rarely for

Malpensa from the central station (Tel: 748 52 200 for information on departure times).

MONEY MATTERS

Most banks open from 8.30am–1.30pm and 2.15pm–3.45pm. Some banks open at different hours. Almost all of them have exchange facilities. The Banca delle Communicazioni in the Stazione Centrale is open longer: Monday to Saturday 8am–9pm. You can also try a 'dispenser', or change machine: they turn foreign currency into lire but not the other way round. At Linate Airport the Banca Popolare di Lodi and the Banca Popolare di Milano are open daily from 8am–9pm including all public holidays except 25 December. The same conditions apply to the Banca Popolare di Milano at Malpensa Airport.

USEFUL INFORMATION

Geography & Topography

Milan, 122m (400ft) above sea level, is the capital of the province of the same name, and also the largest archbishopric in the world.

In 1990 the population within the municipal borders continued to decrease to below 1.4 million. But Greater Milan – made up of 105 municipalities covering 1,224 sq km (470 sq miles) – has a population of over 4 million. It also produces around 25 percent of Italy's GNP, and one quarter of Italy's industry plus countless service industries are based here too.

Milan developed in a series of rings around its historic Roman core. The Roman centre is encircled by the Spanish walls, and around them are the *bastioni*, the outer ring-roads (the bus lines out here are 96 and 97, and tram 29 – see *Pick and Mix* routes 2 and 4).

Weather & Views

In Milan in summer the temperature averages 26-28°C (78-82°F), and in winter 5-11°C (41-52°F). Winter fogs can last an unusually long time, often up to 15 or 20 days a month. The rare breezes tend to come from the south-west. In December and January the sky is usually completely overcast, and it rains sporadically. Snow is very rare. Humidity is high all the year round, as elsewhere in the Lombard Plain.

The one place to get an aerial view of Milan is the roof of the Duomo (tickets on sale outside the Duomo, March to September 9am–5.30pm, October to February 9am–4.30pm). There's a lift up to the roof in the right transept; those keen on climbing the 158 steps need to go to the left transept.

Tourist Information

The **Milan Tourist Information Office** (Tel: 669 03 51) has an office on the platform level of the Central Station (open Monday to Saturday 8am–8pm). The Municipal Railways have a **tourist office** here too: **Ferrovie dello Stato** (Tel: 669 70 32 or 669 70 47). Next to the Duomo, in the Palazzo dell'Arengario, there's the **Azienda Promozione Turistica** APT (Via Marconi 1, Tel: 870 545).

The headquarters of the **Milan Tourist Information Office** is in the Galleria Vittorio Emanuele. Here you can also find the free brochure which gives you important information on the city and also includes a list of events.

The **Centro Turistico Giovanile**, Via S Antonio 2 (Tel: 863 877), caters for young travellers.

Maps

Maps of Milan are available from all stations and airports as well as newsagents and kiosks. They are also obtainable from the tourist information centres (APT) in the Central Station and at Via Marconi 1, as well as from travel agents. The Milan Tourist Office (ATM) also provides topographical maps of Milan. Ask for maps showing the public transport system.

City Round Trips

The **Tourist Information Office** at the Central Station (Tel: 669 04 32) or at Via Marconi 1, and the **Centro Guide Turistiche** (Tel: 86 32 10) organise individual or group trips at varying prices. Guided tours can be booked at several travel agencies as well as at the **Consiglio Autostradale**, which is also open on Sundays and public holidays (Tel: 80 11 61). They do a (multi-lingual) 3-hour-long round trip by bus, beginning at the Piazzetta Reale alongside the Duomo (Tuesday to Saturday 2.30pm, Sunday 10am).

Public Transport

We definitely recommend the use of public transport for our various tours and trips in this guide: driving in Milan means queues, stress and very few parking spaces (and the multi-storeys are expensive).

The offices of the **Azienda Trasporti Municipali (ATM)**, located at the Metro stations 'Duomo' and 'Stazione Centrale', have all the information you'll need.

Tickets & Regulations

You can buy tickets at all Metro stations, newsagents or automatic vending machines, and also in the city's *bartabacchi* (bars that sell tobacco) that display a yellow sign; several kiosks also offer this service.

The **hour-long ticket** *(biglietto orario)* can be used for a (generous) period of 75 minutes on all forms of transport, but only once in the Metro. The tickets need to be stamped in the machines you'll find on the trains and buses.

Then there's the blue **24-hour ticket**, and also the **2-day ticket**; their prices tend to change every few months.

Travelling without a valid ticket can cost up to 30,000 lire in fines.

Children under 1m (3ft) in height travel free, while dogs are only allowed with muzzles. Photography, videos etc. only with prior permission of the ATM press office, Via Foro Buonaparte 61 (Tel: 862 041).

Taxis

The taxis in Milan are yellow (at the Central Station, unauthorised taxi drivers will call out to you, trying to entice you to step inside their vehicles – do not do so on any account). Across the whole city you'll always find a cab at the taxi ranks, which are on most main streets. There's a comprehensive list of ranks in the

pagine gialli (yellow pages).

In an emergency you can ring a radio taxi, and the following should normally turn up:

Ambrosiana Radio Taxi: Tel: 53 53
Arco Radio Taxi: Tel: 67 67
Auto Radio Taxi: Tel: 85 85
Esperia Radio Taxi: Tel: 83 88

The basic rate is 4,000 lire, and 850 lire per kilometre after that, or 21,000 lire an hour. Holiday surcharge is 1,000 lire on top of the basic rate, night surcharge after 10.30pm is 10 percent extra.

Hire Cars

The *pagine gialli* (yellow pages) contain a lot of possibilities including the following:

AUTORENT
Garage Palace, Piazza della Repubblica 20, Tel: 65 02 13

AVIS
Via Fabio Filzi 43, Tel: 69 81

EURODRIVE
Piazza della Repubblica 27, Tel: 670 45 82

EUROPCAR
Via Galvani 12, Tel: 607 10 51

Cycling

The best advice for those planning to explore Milan by bike is don't.The car is king in Milan, and it spares neither pedestrians nor cyclists. If you really feel like cycling, there are a few things you should know: the city has 23km (14 miles) of cycle lanes, but, although well laid out, they're usually totally blocked by parked cars or bags full of rubbish. You can get more information on cycle lanes and routes from the Municipality of Milan Information Office in the Galleria Vittorio Emanuele.
Bicycle hire: Available in the city centre at the Piazza Fontana, Piazza San Babila, Piazza Cadorna, Piazza

Oberdan, Corso Garibaldi, Largo Cairoli, Piazza S Eustorgio (Monday to Friday 9.30am–6pm). Outside the city centre: Parco Monza Tel: (039) 202 03 15; Parco nel Ticino Tel: 975 43 46 (business hours vary). Rental prices are usually reasonable; bring your passport along too for identification.

A good place to cycle is the Parco di Trenno in S Siro, or around the Parco Sempione. Use the maps they give you when you hire the bike.

And What About Pedestrians?

The rules are the same here as in all other major cities: be extremely careful at traffic lights and zebra crossings (or pedestrian crossings of any description), particularly if you have children with you. Even when the light is green, take an extra look around – and make sure you reach the safety of the other side as quickly as possible. Pedestrian paradise is to be found in the car-free zone around the Duomo.

ACCOMMODATION

If you're planning to stay the night in Milan, expect accommodation problems from the word go. Spontaneous visits can often end up on a park bench, mainly because Milan is almost always hosting some exhibition or other, and whenever it does so the hotels are fully booked.

Hotel reservations are best done via a travel agent before departure. Here's a magic phone number, though, for those who don't want to be tied down:

Hotel Reservation Milan, Via Palestro 24, Tel: 70 60 95, which makes reservations for 3-star hotels upwards. Rooms can also be obtained via the APT information office, Via Marconi 1 (near the Duomo), Tel: 87 00 16 or 80 96 62.

Ask whether VAT (*Iva*) and breakfast are included in the price. The rates mentioned below are based on double rooms. So here is my list of recommended hotels that still treat their guests like guests:

5-Star & Luxury Hotels
500,000 to 640,000 lire

EXCELSIOR GALLIA
Piazza Duca d'Aosta, Tel: 62 77
Renovated, one of the best hotels in the world, conference rooms.

GRAND HOTEL BRUN
Via Caldera 21, Tel: 45 271
Transfers from and to the airport.

PALACE
Piazza della Repubblica 20
Tel: 63 36
In the centre, renovated, roof garden with fine view, babysitter service.

PRINCIPE DI SAVOIA
Piazza della Repubblica 17
Tel: 62 30
An antique gem, luxury suites (Frank Sinatra is a regular), private garage.

4-Star Hotels
150,000 lire to 500,000 lire

CAPITOL
Via Cimarosa 6, Tel: 498 88 51
Well situated for trade fair visitors.

CARLTON
Via Senato 5, Tel: 79 85 83
Definitely to be recommended: quiet, and opposite the national monument.

MANIN
Via Manin 7/8, Tel: 659 65 11
Next to the Giardini Pubblici, quiet atmosphere, attractive and modern rooms.

EXECUTIVE
Viale Sturzo 45, Tel: 62 94
A brand-new hotel with sound-proofed rooms near the Stazione Garibaldi.

MICHELANGELO
Via Scarlatti 33, Tel: 67 55
Very modern hotel near the Central Station with 250 rooms, brunch, conference rooms.

3-/2-/1-Star Hotels
60,000 to 100,000 lire

ANDREOLA
Via Scarlatti 41, Tel: 670 91 41
100 metres away from the Central Station and bus stops for Linate and Malpensa airports. Colour TV with satellite and international channels, garage.

ANTICA LOCANDA SOLFERINO
Via Castelfidardo 2, Tel: 65 96 05
Situated in the Brera.

ARIOSTO
Via Ariosto 22, Tel: 49 09 95
Near the trade fair centre; rooms with view of a fine garden.

BISCIONE
Via S Maria Fulcorina 15
Tel: 879 903
City centre; facilities for the disabled.

CESARE CORRENTI
Via Cesare Correnti 14, Tel: 87 07 25
In the city centre.

EUROPEO
Via Canonica 38, Tel: 331 47 51
Near trade fair centre; one of the few hotels in Milan with a garden and a pool.

GRAN DUCA DI YORK
Via Moneta 1a, Tel: 87 48 63
Near the Pinacoteca Brera in an old *palazzo*.

PALAZZO DELLE STELLINE
Corso Magenta 61, Tel: 481 85 03
Very new, part of the large congress centre; facilities for the disabled.

Campsites
AGIP
In Metanopoli S. Donato Milanese; access via the Autostrada del Soleaperto
Open all year; tents and caravans.

BAREGGINO
In Bareggio
Caravans and tents.

MONZA
In the park at Monza
Tel: (039) 387 771
Open 1 April to 30 September. Caravans, tents, campers; covered swimming pool, bar and grocery store.

Youth Hostels
OSTELLO ROTTA
Via Martino Bassi 2, Tel: 367 095
Depart 7am–9am, return 5pm–11pm.

BUSINESS HOURS

Apart from food shops, most of the city's shops are open 9am–1pm and 3.30pm–7.30pm. Nearly all the shops are closed on Monday morning.

EMERGENCIES

In case of emergency
SOS emergency number: Tel: 113
Carabinieri 'pronto intervento': Tel: 112
Fire Brigade: Tel: 115
City Police: Tel: 772 71
Emergency Medical Aid: Tel: 3883
Traffic Police: Tel: 32 67 81
Towed-Away Car Lot: Tel: 77 33

Breakdown Services
ACI (Automobil Club Italiano), Tel: 774 51; serious accidents, Tel: 352 02 91
ACI Breakdown Service: Tel: 116
Autofficina Autostrada Nord: Viale Certosa 223, Tel: 308 37 24. Open all day, all year round.
Autofficina Locatelli: Via Tolstoi 22/12, Tel: 48 95 05 45
Autofficina Boschetti: Via del Ghisallo 9, Tel: 38 00 73 33
Autofficina Pomezia: Via Venini 38/8, Tel: 282 20 23
Autofficina Pavese: Via Naviglio Pavese 10, Tel: 581 11 869

Medical Assistance
Assistenza Medicine Salute Sanità: Tel: 166 21 64. Medical information service for foreigners not resident in Italy.
AIDS hotline: Tel: 62 08 70 70 or 62 08 68 06
Alcoholics Anonymous: Tel: 71 36

62 or 688 81 91

Emergency Dental Treatment: Tel: 86 54 60, 24 hours.

Niguarda Drugs Helpline: Tel: 64 44 26 52 or 64 44 24 52

Emergency Pharmacies

24-hour: Piazza Duomo, Via Orefici 2, Central Station (departure hall).

9pm–8.30am: Bracco, Via Boccaccio 26; Ticinese, Corso S. Gottardo 1; Venezia, Corso Buenos Aires 4; Carrobbio, Corso Genova 23.

Hospital Out-Patient Service

Niguarda: Piazza Ospedale Maggiore 3, Tel: 64 44 24 96

Policlinico: Via Francesco Sforza 35, Tel: 551 16 55

Fatebenefratelli: Corso Porta Nuova 23, Tel: 636 34 699

San Raffaele: Via Olgettina 60, Tel: 26 43 27 41

Ortopedico Pini: Piazza Cardinal Ferrari 1, Tel: 58 38 01

Emergency Veterinary Service

Ambulanza Veterinaria: Tel: 545 13 98

Ambulatorio Bessarione: Tel: 569 60 97

Night Service: Tel: 88 11

Pronto soccorso Brera: Tel: 657 29 03

Lost & Found

Central Station: Tel: 677 12 577

Linate Airport: Tel: 738 44 51

Malpensa Airport: Tel: 748 54 215

Trams, Metro: Via Unione 4, Monday to Friday 8.30am–12.45pm, 2.15pm–5pm, Saturday 8.30am–noon

MEDIA

Newspapers

Every newspaper in Milan contains a supplement or a special page with a list of events.

The main newspapers are *Corriere della Sera, Repubblica, L'Unita, Il Giorno, Il Giornale,* and *La Notte. La Repubblica* certainly has the biggest services section (not on Mondays). The Italian equivalent of *Exchange & Mart* is *Seconda Mano*, which comes out on Monday, Wednesday and Friday.

Television

The TV market in Italy is shared between public stations (RAI 1, RAI 2, RAI 3) and private ones. There are a huge amount of private stations, some of which, however, are of national importance e.g. Berlusconi's stations (Italia 1, Rete 4 and Canale 5). The main local stations in Milan are Telelombardia, Lombardia 7 TV, Telenova and Antenna 3.

Radio

There are 170 radio stations sharing the ether above Milan. Since there's no law governing transmission frequencies the stations often tend to overlap. The result? Total chaos. Here's a brief list of the more audible ones: Radio Popolare (107 MHz) is a 24-hour news station; Radio Montestella (103.2 MHz) is a mixture of news and music; Radio Milano International (101 MHz) plays American music and has a news service; Radio Meneghina (92.2 MHz) plays Milanese songs and gives local reports.

POST & TELECOMMUNICATIONS

Telephoning

The area code for Milan is 02.
Most phone boxes have been changed over to the card system now, and cards can be bought in *bar tabacchi* or at newsstands. To dial other countries first dial the international access code 00, then the country code: Australia (61); France (33); Germany (49); Japan (81); Netherlands (31); Spain (34); UK (44); US and Canada (1). If using a US credit phone card, dial the company's access number below – Sprint, Tel: 172 1877; AT&T, Tel: 172 1011; MCI, Tel: 172 1022. Public telephones are plentiful at the Central Station, the Galleria Vittorio Emanuele and the Piazza Cordusio.

Post Offices

The main post office in the city *(poste centrale)* is at Piazza Cordusio 1. Postal services are available weekdays 8.30am–5.30pm. Registered letters, parcels and *poste restante* can be handed in or collected at Via Cordusio 4 (weekdays 8.15am–7.40pm, and until 5.40pm on Saturday and public holidays).

There are more large post offices at the Central Station and at the airports. Milanese letter-boxes are red and have two slots, one for the city and the other for outside. The orange letter boxes are for letters that need to reach their recipients in the city within one day (or so you hope): this *servizio postacelere* costs extra.

Telegrams, telexes and telefaxes can be sent off and received round the clock in the Posta Centrale, Via Cordusio 4.

For Children

Milan has a great deal to offer old

and young alike.
Babysitter service, *Via Vittadini 3, Tel: 54 54 54.*
Babysitters aged between 19 and 50 look after children from 0 to 12. Minimum booking period ranges from 2 hours to whole days and nights. The babysitters look after the children's clothes too.
ABIO, *Via Commenda 9, Tel: 545 32 76.*
The qualified personnel here are specialists at keeping children happy.
Citta del Sole, *Via Dante 13.* The only really good

toy shop in Milan – no electronic toys.
Gog & Magog, *Via Canonica 13.*
Educational games, intelligent free-time ideas.
Libreria dei Ragazzi, *Via Unione 3.*
Educational toys.
Motta Baby, *Viale Montenero 22.*
A huge shop with children's furniture.
Arci Ragazzi, *Via Mario Fanti 19.*
Organises holiday activities and camps for children.
Teatro del Buratto, *Sala Don Orione, Via Fezzan.*
Performances (musicals, puppet shows, etc).
Teatro delle Marionette, *Via Olive-tani 3b.*
Not to be missed: Gianni and Cosetta Colla's puppets fascinate children of all ages (Grimms' fairy tales, Hans Andersen, etc).

Teatro Gnomo, *Via Lanzone 30a*.
Theatre, ballet, cinema.
Luna Park Varesine, *Viale ex Varesine*.
This mini-Disneyland is not only of interest to children: there's a great smell of doughnuts and very loud disco music.
Cinema Eliseo, *Via Torino 46*.
Matinée cinema for children and young people.

For Women

CICIP E CICIAP, *Via Morigi 8*.
Open until 1am. A bar and restaurant just for women, in an old Milanese *palazzo*: young students and middle-aged women can gather here unpestered and play the guitar or attend various other courses.

For The Disabled

Lega per i diritti handicappati (Association for Rights of the Disabled), *Tel: 54 52 444*.
All information on provisions for the disabled in Milan is available here.

SPORT

In Milan you can engage in practically any sport, where and when you like. Telephone numbers aren't always provided below – just check in the *pagine gialli* (yellow pages).

Boccia

A popular sport in Milan, which has produced several world champions.
Bocciodromo Comunale, *Via Candiani 7*.
Nuovo Bocciodromo, *Via Missaglia 46/3*.
Grand Hotel Pub, *Via Ascanio Sforzo 75*.

Bowling

Bowling Corvetto, *Via Mario d'Agrate 23*.

Boccia is Milan's favourite sport

Bowling dei Fiori, *Via Renzo e Lucia 4, Via Arona 19*.

Tennis

CMSR, *Piazzale Lotto 15, Tel: 39 16 67*. For keen beginners.
Tennis Club Ambrosiano, *Via Feltre 33*. 19 courts for experts.
Tennis Club Bonacossa, *Via Arimondi 15*.

Canoeing

Canottieri Olona, *at the swimming baths on the Via Alzaia/Naviglio Grande 146, Tel: 48 95 23 46*.

Riding

Centro Ippico Borromeo, *S Felice, Tel: 753 16 26*.

Golf

Federazione Golf, *Via Canonica 5, Tel: 799 02 40*
Lucchesi Peschiera Borromeo, *Via Lombardia*
Parco di Monza, *Tel: (039) 30 31 81*. 18-hole course.

Indoor Swimming Pools

Cozzi, *Viale Tunisia 35*
Solari im Park, *Via Coni Zugna*

Outdoor Swimming Pools

Argelati, *Via Sgantini 6*
Scarioni, *Via Valfurva 9*
Canottieri Olona (see above): the best pool in Milan.

Jogging ('Footing')

Giardino Villa Litta, 800m (2,624ft) course.

Monte Stella, up and down this artificial mountain near S Siro.

Parco Sempione, 2,240 metres (7,300 ft) through the park.

USEFUL ADDRESSES

Kiosks Open At Night

Corso Buenos Aires 4 (until 2am)
Galleria Vittorio Emanuele (24 hours)
Piazza Oberdan, near the Porta Venezia (24 hours)
Via Larga (until 2 am)

Consulates

There are more than 80 consulates in Milan. Check through the yellow pages under *consolati* to get the addresses and phone numbers.

Foreign Cultural Institutes

British Council
Via Manzoni 38, Tel: 78 20 16
Centre Culturel Français
Via Bigli 2, Tel: 76 01 39 66
Goethe Institut Milan
Via S. Paolo 10, Tel: 78 34 74
United States IS
Via Bigli 11a, Tel: 79 50 53

Airlines

Air France
Piazza Cavour 2, Tel: 77 38 1
Alitalia
Via Albricci 5, Tel: 628 17
Austrian Airlines
Piazza Diaz 5, Tel: 80 77 94
British Airways
Corso Italia 8, Tel: 80 90 41
KLM
Via Paolo da Cannobio 33, Tel: 86 64 41
Lufthansa
Via Larga 23, Tel: 855 81

SAS
Via Albricci 7, Tel: 86 75 41

Banks

Credito Italiano, *Piazza XXIV Maggio*. The only bank open Thursday until 6pm.
Dresdner Bank, *Piazza Affari 3*
Crédit Lyonnais, *Via Borgonuovo 18*
Creditanstalt, *Via Maria Teresa 11*
Chase Manhattan Bank, *Piazza Meda 1*
National Westminster Bank, *Via S Margherita 7*

Travel Agencies

Ente Provinciale del Turismo
Via Marconi 1
This city travel agency is very helpful for general queries about Milan.
Centro Turistico Giovanile
Via S Angelo 2, Tel: 86 38 77
Itinerari nel Mondo
Via Camperio 14, Tel: 80 10 91
Third world travel specialists.
CIT
Galleria Vittorio Emanuele, Tel: 86 66 61
American Express
Via Brera, Tel: 855 71
Chi Arriva
Via Dante 8, Tel: 850 41

Advance Ticket Sales

Showticket, *Piazza Duomo* in the *Virgin Megastore Duomo Centre* (Tel: 72 00 33 70, Tuesday to Saturday 10am–midnight, Sunday and Monday noon–10pm). Tickets for all types of event, including foreign ones.

APT **(Azienda Promozione Turistica)**, *Piazza Marconi 1, Tel: 800 16 or 80 96 62.*

Art & Photo Credits

Photography	**Sergio Piumatti** *and*
Pages 10, 11, 27, 28, 44, 45	**Scala/Firenze**
12	**La Repubblica/Alinari**
Publisher	**Hans Höfer**
Design Concept	**V Barl**
Designer	**Gaia Text, Munich**
Managing Editor	**Andrew Eames**
Cartography	**Berndtson & Berndtson**

Milan's Metro Network

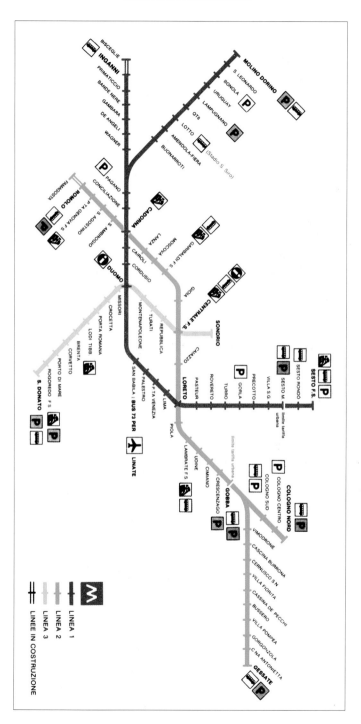

INSIGHT GUIDES

COLORSET NUMBERS

You'll find the colorset number on the spine of each Insight Guide.

INSIGHT *pocket* GUIDES

EXISTING & FORTHCOMING TITLES:

• •

United States: **Houghton Mifflin Company, Boston MA 02108**
Tel: (800) 2253362 Fax: (800) 4589501

Canada: **Thomas Allen & Son, 390 Steelcase Road East**
Markham, Ontario L3R 1G2
Tel: (416) 4759126 Fax: (416) 4756747

Great Britain: **GeoCenter UK, Hampshire RG22 4BJ**
Tel: (256) 817987 Fax: (256) 817988

Worldwide: **Höfer Communications Singapore 2262**
Tel: (65) 8612755 Fax: (65) 8616438

" I was first drawn to the Insight Guides by the excellent "Nepal" volume. I can think of no book which so effectively captures the essence of a country. Out of these pages leaped the Nepal I know – the captivating charm of a people and their culture. I've since discovered and enjoyed the entire Insight Guide Series. Each volume deals with a country or city in the same sensitive depth, which is nowhere more evident than in the superb photography. "

Sir Edmund Hillary

NOTES